How To Start A Bail Bond Business And Become A Bail Bondsman

....

A Step-By-Step Success Formula

By

Richard Verrochi, CBA

....

Find out <u>exactly</u> how to start your Bail Bond Business Successfully!

ISBN 978-0-9789569-1-2

This work is dedicated to

the three most important people in my life:

Christine, Nicole and Katherine

And to

Judi Aultman, who put me into the

Bail Bond Business so many years ago.

Table of Contents

Disclaimer...1

A Note On Gender Specific References.................................2

About The Author...3

Introduction...5

     Why I Wrote This Book...5

Why Do We Need Bail Agents?..7

     The Role of Bail Agents...7

     The Moral Decision Versus The Financial Decision.......8

A Short History of Bail...9

     Bail As Hostage-Taking In Ancient Times......................9

     Old English Law...9

     Eighth Amendment to the US Constitution....................10

     The Bail Agent's Right of Arrest....................................11

How Bail Works..13

     Arrest..13

     Bail Commissioner/Arraignment in Court.....................13

     Bail Schedules..14

     Typical Crimes...14

     Bond (Not Cash) Posted..15

Bail as a Lifestyle...17

     The Entrepreneurial Spirit and Acceptance of Risk......17

     Minimum Initial Cash Investment.................................18

     Role in the Criminal Justice System..............................18

Obligations of the Bail Agent...19

How The Industry Is Organized.......................................21

    Surety Agents and Property Bondsmen......................21

    Surety Insurance Company...23

    Contract With Surety Company....................................23

    Where To Find A Surety Company...............................25

    Managing General Agent..27

    General Agent...27

    Sub-Agent...28

    Direct Writer...28

    Liable Versus Non-Liable Agents................................29

Bail Statutes In Your State...30

    Review of Your State's Statutes...................................30

    Requirements For Licensing..31

    Regulations By Regulating Department......................31

    Rules For Forfeiting Bail...31

    Basis to Vacate Forfeiture..32

Licensing..34

    Regulation of the Business...34

    Fidelity Bond..35

    Appointment by Sheriff for Property Bondsmen........36

    Appointment by Insurance Department.......................36

    Bail Enforcement Agent (Bounty Hunter).................37

Understanding the Bail Markets.......................................39

    Size of Statewide Markets..39

    Most Competitive Markets...40

"No Bail" States………………………………………………………41

Federal Bonds……………………………………………………42

Terminology……………………………………………………………43

Defendant or Principal……………………………………………...43

Obligor…………………………………………………………44

Obligee…………………………………………………………44

Surety…………………………………………………………44

Indemnitor………………………………………………………45

Underwriting Guidelines…………………………………………45

Bail Bond Fee……………………………………………………45

Collateral………………………………………………………45

Bond Cost………………………………………………………46

Build-Up Fund (BUF)……………………………………………46

Cash Only Bail……………………………………………………46

Personal Recognizance……………………………………………...47

Credit Bonding and Time Payments………………………………47

Jails Versus Prisons………………………………………………47

Forfeiture………………………………………………………48

Revocation………………………………………………………48

Remission………………………………………………………48

Bail Enforcement Agent…………………………………………48

Discharge or Exoneration…………………………………………49

Appearance Versus Performance Bond……………………………49

Posting Fee………………………………………………………49

Women In Bail………………………………………………………50

Many Women Own Bail Agencies………………………………50

14000 Agents In US, 48% Are Women.................................51

Are Women Better Than Men?....................................51

Is It Safe?...52

Establishing Your Bail Bond Business.................................53

Is Bail Viable In Your Area?.....................................53

To Buy Or To Start New?.......................................53

Naming Your Business...55

Corporation or Sole Proprietorship..............................56

Insurance..56

An Office Versus A Telephone Number?..........................57

Getting Your Name Posted At The Jail..........................57

Equipment...58

Become A Credit Card Merchant................................59

Check Guarantee Service..60

Your Business Briefcase...62

Forms...62

Camera...63

Credit Card Machine and Charge Slips..........................64

Miscellaneous...65

Steps In The Posting Of A Bail Bond.................................66

Discuss Defendant With Indemnitor.............................66

Underwriting..66

Negotiate Fee and Collateral....................................67

Meet Indemnitor, Receive Fee and Collateral....................69

Interview The Defendant At The Jail............................69

Post The Bond At The Court Or Jail............................70

Defendant Is Released...71

Day-To-Day Business Operations...................................72

Develop Clear Underwriting Guidelines.........................72

Monitoring...73

Accounting System..74

Employees Or Subcontractors?.....................................74

Financial Accounts And Cash Collateral.........................76

Non-Cash Collateral..77

Reporting Requirements..77

Importance of Bond Discharges....................................78

Management of Client Data..79

Advertising And Promotion..80

Yellow Pages...80

Used U-Haul Trucks...81

Jail Postings And Sign Boards......................................82

Collect Calls And Toll-Free Numbers..............................82

Billboards...83

Internet..84

Bumper Stickers...84

Give-Aways...85

Community Networking...86

Rewards For Fugitives And Wanted Posters......................87

Going To The Courthouse With A Big Check......................89

When It All Goes Wrong..91

"If You Write Bail, You Will Have Forfeitures"..................91

Bail Enforcement Agent (Bounty Hunter).........................92

Extradition Limitations…………………………………94

Making Your Business Grow…………………………………96

Agents And Sub-Agents…………………………………96

The Owner Should NOT Run The Business…………………………97

Other Bonding Opportunities…………………………………99

Immigration Bonds…………………………………99

Court Bonds…………………………………100

Child Custody Bonds…………………………………101

Visa Bonds And Guest Worker Bonds…………………………101

Related Businesses…………………………………103

GPS Tracking…………………………………103

Electronic Monitoring…………………………………104

Drug/Alcohol/DNA Testing…………………………………105

Western Union…………………………………106

Check Cashing And Payday Loans…………………………106

Electronic Filing/Tax Preparation…………………………107

A General Comment About Related Businesses………………108

Associations, Education, And Networking……………………109

Professional Bail Agents of The United States………………109

State-Wide And Local Associations………………………110

Surety Company Conventions…………………………111

Valuing And Selling Your Bail Agency……………………113

To Whom Can You Sell?…………………………………113

To Whom Should You Sell?………………………………114

What's It Worth?…………………………………115

If You REALLY, REALLY Need To Sell Now…………………116

Miscellaneous Contacts..117

A Short List Of Surety Companies And Contacts...............................120

Forms

Appendix

Disclaimer

Although every effort has been made to check, re-check, verify and confirm the information contained in this work, it is incumbent upon the reader to consult with competent legal and accounting professionals before attempting to implement any or all of the information provided herein.

A good faith effort has been made to provide factual information and documents, but the world changes daily, and mistakes do occur. The author cannot accept responsibility for the use or misuse of this material.

This work is subject to change without notice, is copyrighted, and all rights are reserved to the author. No portion of this work, in whole or in part, may be copied or transmitted by any means, electronic or mechanical, without the express written permission of the copyright holder.

- 1 -

A Note On Gender Specific References

As the father of two successful young women, I appreciate the importance of gender neutrality in all writing. All references to "he" or "him" in this work are designed to be more convenient than writing "he or she" and "him or her" repeatedly through the book.

I ask for the indulgence and understanding of my female readers.

Also, please note the chapter **Women in Bail**. In my experience, I have found women to have a better underwriting sense or "sixth sense" than men regarding whether or not to bail a defendant.

As my daughters remind me, women *will* end up ruling the world!

About The Author

Whenever I read a non-fiction work, I want to know that the author really knows what he is talking and writing about. For that reason, I would like to tell you just a little bit about both my professional and political life.

For seventeen years, I was a Stockbroker, selling stocks, bonds and mutual funds for some of the largest firms on Wall Street. During the last few years of that career, I realized that I was neither a salesman, nor a "company man". What I needed was a business of my own.

As you will read further on in this work, my interest in bail resulted in the beginnings of a new business in 1993, in New Hampshire. I started as a single Bail Bondsman, establishing Amherst Bail Bonds, Inc., a company that still exists today. Soon I was hiring employees, sub-agents, and expanding statewide and even beyond the borders of New Hampshire. Eventually, Amherst Bail Bonds, Inc. came to be the largest bail bond agency in Northern New England.

I became involved on the national scene with the Professional Bail Agents of the United States (PBUS) www.pbus.com, received the professional designation of Certified Bail Agent (CBA) and became Education Chairman, Editor of the magazine *The Bail Agent's Perspective*, Director, and eventually President.

I have traveled extensively to speak and consult with bail agents and state organizations across the country.

It was my privilege to represent the bail bond business as President of PBUS, speaking before the United States Congress, in hearings on federal bail legislation.

In my political life, I served as Selectman in my Town for twelve years and ran twice for County Commissioner (I lost both times). I also served the State of New Hampshire as Real Estate Commissioner for thirteen years.

My intent in this work is to fully share my bail bond experience with you, and to introduce you to a wonderful business!

Introduction

Why I Wrote This Book

In the 1980's, I became very interested in establishing a bail bond agency. Living in a section of the country where the bail market was relatively small and inactive, I found that there were no opportunities to learn the intricacies of the business. Even the *Readers' Guide* at the local library was of little help, listing only one book, which was out-of-print. Remember, these were the pre-internet days.

The library did, however, have copies of the *Yellow Pages* from various parts of the country. So, I began calling bail agencies that were hundreds, in some cases thousands, of miles away, trying to learn about bail. Finally, a kind-hearted Bondsman referred me to a surety insurance company in California, where I was able to talk with one of the regional managers about starting a bail bond agency.

From that telephone call, I learned that surety insurance companies are very reluctant to sign a contract with anyone who has not had some experience in the bail business (that attitude has changed today). However, I was eventually able to convince this regional manager to meet with me to discuss my desire to be in bail.

That meeting resulted in my contracting with the surety company, and started me on the road to success in the bail bond business.

What I did not realize at the time was that my contract was an anomaly, a real exception to the rule. Years later, that regional manager told me that I was one of only two "greenies" whom she ever took into the business.

Now that I had a contract, I had to go through all of the intricacies of licensing and establishing my bail bond agency with little or no guidance. How was I to proceed?

There was no manual, document or book that could educate me on bail. The surety company was able to provide me with forms, but that was about all of the support that I received, except for some telephone guidance from the regional manager.

Everything that I did was trial-and-error, where I learned from my mistakes. But I came to love bail, in a way that I have never before loved a profession.

Having come through the start-up, growth, expansion and final sale of my bail bond business, I felt the need to try to help all of those people who want to learn about bail.

This book is designed to be as comprehensive as possible, containing extensive explanations of the nuances of the business, along with sample forms and appended documents to help you establish your business.

I am very pleased to welcome you to the business that I love. I wish you a hugely successful career in bail!

Why Do We Need Bail Agents?

The Role of Bail Agents

Guarantee of Appearance – First and foremost, a Bail Agent provides a financial guarantee that a defendant will appear in court for trial. Given the presumption of innocence upon which our criminal justice system is based, a defendant can be released from jail to help prepare his defense and to get along with supporting his family. With release from jail, there is an inherent risk that the defendant will abscond and fail to appear for trial. The Bail Agent provides the guarantee to the court that the defendant will appear.

Financial Assistance to Families in Need – Most families are unable to produce on short notice the thousands of dollars that may be necessary to post bail for a defendant. The Bail Agent steps into this gap, acting as a financial intermediary, by posting a bond to guarantee the defendant's appearance. In this way, families can be reunited, court defenses prepared, and financial support continued.

Jail Overcrowding – A chronic problem for today's communities is the overcrowding of local jails. Many federal court decisions have been handed down ordering the expansion of local jails, or the release of prisoners. Both of these alternatives may be unacceptable to a community. Bail Agents provide the release of defendants and reduction of jail overcrowding, while still guaranteeing the appearances in court.

The Moral Decision Versus The Financial Decision

Many people question the morality of being a Bail Agent, in that you are assisting in the release back into society of a defendant who might be charged with very serious crimes.

There have been times when I have walked away from a bail because I really did believe the defendant was dangerous. However, the moral decision whether or not to release a defendant is always made by the judge in the courtroom. The size and type of bail set by the judge is a reflection of society's view of the crime and the defendant. The Bail Agent merely implements that already-made decision.

Cash Only, Surety or Personal Recognizance Bail? As discussed in detail in the following chapters, not only the amount, but also the type of bail is a further consideration in the judge's decision. The type of bail reflects the ease with which a defendant can be released.

A Short History of Bail

Bail as Hostage-Taking In Ancient Times

Many historians and other writers trace the evolution of bail back to early Biblical times or before, when a tribal leader's children or other family members would be given to an opposing tribe as a guarantee of the peace, or some other such agreement. In the event that the agreement was breached, the hostages would be killed. For a parent, this would be a pretty strong motivation to abide by the agreement.

Old English Law

During the Middle Ages, a defendant in England would be tried by a Magistrate riding a court circuit through the countryside. Because of the distances and modes of travel, a Magistrate might appear in a town or village only once each year. The problem for the local sheriff was simple: what do you do with the defendant while waiting many months for the Magistrate?

A system of personal guarantee evolved. A family member or friend would guarantee that the defendant would appear before the Magistrate, or the guarantor would pay a severe penalty. Initially, the penalty was simple: if the defendant failed to appear, the guarantor would take the place of the defendant and be tried and sentenced for the defendant's crimes.

Given the severity of the penalty to the guarantor when the defendant failed to appear, many people refused to make this sometimes life-threatening guarantee. Over time, the guarantee became property-based (so many pigs, horses or perhaps your land). Eventually, as currency became more advanced, the penalty was purely financial.

Eighth Amendment to the US Constitution

From these early English roots, American settlers adopted many of the common methods of law, including the English Bill of Rights. When our nation was founded, the Bill of Rights, making up the first ten amendments to the constitution, was quickly enacted.

The Eight Amendment to the US Constitution reads as follows:

"Excessive bail shall not be required, nor excessive fines imposed, nor cruel and unusual punishments inflicted."

Through more than two hundred and forty years of American constitutional litigation, there have been many cases involving the Eighth Amendment. However, the right to bail is a fundamental right that has been continuously defended, except for capital cases.

The Bail Agent's Right of Arrest

Along with the English notion of the right to bail came certain protections for a person who acted as a surety (the technical name for the guarantor).

In the English system of law, a surety could return the defendant to the sheriff to be remanded back into the local jail. The logic here is that the defendant had been released into the custody of the surety, and the surety could release himself of obligation by surrendering the defendant. Thus, a surety who felt that the defendant was about to abscond could arrest and surrender him to the sheriff.

The right of the surety to arrest and surrender the defendant descended into American law and was clearly stated in the US Supreme Court's decision <u>Taylor v. Taintor (1872, 83 U.S. 366 Wall).</u> The most often cited section of this decision is:

> *"When bail is given, the principal is regarded as delivered to the custody of his sureties. Their dominion is a continuance of the original imprisonment. Whenever they choose to do so, they may seize him and deliver him up in their discharge; and if that cannot be done at once, they may imprison him until it can be done. They may exercise their rights in person or by agent. They may pursue him into another State; may arrest him on the Sabbath; and, if necessary, may break and enter his house for that purpose. The seizure is not made by virtue of new process. None is needed. It is likened to the rearrest by the sheriff of an escaping prisoner...The bail have their principal on a string, and may pull the string whenever they please, and render him in their discharge..."*

It is important not to take these words in their most literal sense. Many states have legislated and reinterpreted these words to put limitations on the great power granted here to a surety. However, this decision still remains as the seminal and definitive opinion on the rights of the surety in the United States.

Discretion in the exercise of this power of arrest is necessary to avoid the perception by the court and the public that bail was revoked in an arbitrary or capricious manner.

I tried hard to never bail a defendant for a "girlfriend" or a "boyfriend", because the relationship could end tomorrow and there would be a resultant demand to me to revoke the defendant's bail. However, if someone failed to appear in court, or the house that I had as collateral was about to be foreclosed, there was never a hesitation in my decision to dispatch my bail recovery agents.

How Bail Works

Arrest

When a defendant is arrested, he or she begins a long road to the final disposition of the case. It can take months, or even years, before this criminal matter has been fully adjudicated. Whenever I wrote a bond, I expected that the case would take a year to be complete, but the average seemed to be in the four to six month range.

The "ride downtown" usually means a trip to the local police station, and then transfer to the local jail. After being "booked" (fingerprints, picture, basic personal/identification information), the defendant has the first of a small number of assessment interviews, including the Bail Commissioner.

Bail Commissioner/Arraignment In Court

Depending upon the state and the individual jurisdiction, the defendant may be held in jail until the next business day to be arraigned in court in front of a judge or magistrate where bail will be set.

Alternatively, to reduce the court workload and expedite the bailing of defendants, a Bail Commissioner may do an interview and set bail. The job of the Bail Commissioner, as an officer of the court, is to set and receive bail for defendants who have been recently arrested. Typically, the defendant or the person posting bail will pay a Bail Commissioner's fee, which is in the range of $25 to $50. How does the Bail Commissioner set the bail?

Bail Schedules

Many states have very specific bail schedules, established statewide or by county. The schedule may call for a DWI bail to be set at $500, while a sexual assault might be $25,000.

Other states and local courts leave the setting of bail to the Bail Commissioner's discretion, based upon his interview of the defendant.

Typical Crimes

The types of crimes that you will deal with cover the complete gamut. They can be drunken fights among friends, or pre-planned stabbings among enemies. What you will see will vary by geography.

When most people think of crime, they envision the gangs of Los Angeles, the street crimes of New York City, or the drug smuggling of the Southwest.

If you begin your business in one of the urban centers of our country, yes, you will see all of these types of violent and drug-related crime. Your business will be much busier, and your average bail will be much higher. However, the risk of numerous failures to appear (FTA's) will also have an impact on the success of your business.

In a more rural environment, such as Idaho, Montana, the Dakotas, etc., the types of crime will change. Your basic business will revolve around domestic violence, alcohol and drug usage. I used to make a very crass joke: "If it weren't for booze, drugs and marriage, I would be out of business".

You need to carefully assess what types of crime occur in your area, and what the relative risk level is for a bail bond business. When I first began my business, some local police and lawyer friends were shocked. I can remember one local court clerk who said to me, "You'll go broke! No one ever shows up for court!" We will talk about this common misperception further in this work.

Bond (Not Cash) Posted

Many people are familiar with posting a few hundred dollars cash bail for a child, friend or employee who has run afoul of the law. There is a quick trip to the ATM, a fast drive to the jail, and then lots of heckling of the defendant who was released.

When I was called to the jail, I carried a large catalogue-style briefcase to hold all of my forms, camera, credit card equipment, etc. The

Bail Commissioners and I would meet in a small conference room to sign the bail bond and the other necessary forms to release the defendant.

I don't know how many times I was asked the question, "Aren't you nervous carrying around that big bag of money?" I was shocked that even jail personnel thought that I was giving the Bail Commissioner cash to arrange the release of the defendant.

A bail agent gives the court or bail commissioner a bond, a written guarantee, that if the defendant does not appear, and the bail agent is unable to produce him, the bail agent will pay the forfeited bail.

I believe that much of the personal mystique that seems to develop around a bail agent comes from the belief that the "big bag" is filled with cash!

Bail as a Lifestyle

The Entrepreneurial Spirit and Acceptance of Risk

The Entrepreneurial Spirit is really embodied in the bail bond business. It is the quintessential start-up business that involves more risk than the typical new venture. As will be explained later in this work, you become personally responsible for each and every bail bond that you write, and you must be able to feel comfortable with that responsibility.

There is an old saying about businesses involving risk: "You can either eat well, or sleep well". As you begin to develop your own guidelines regarding for whom you will post bail, you will be making this decision between money today or sleeping tonight.

This is a business in which you are your own boss, which really means that you have no one to fall back upon when things start going wrong. The opposite side of the coin is that you will enjoy being the person who makes the final decisions, knowing that you are deciding your own fate.

I could write pages and pages about why you should be your own boss, but this is a "How To" book, not a "Why You Should Do It" book.

Minimum Initial Cash Investment

Many businesses require the purchase of extensive equipment, real estate, franchise purchase costs, on-going franchise fees, and the hiring of many employees.

The bail bond business is different.

When we get to the sections about surety companies, licensing and cash deposits, you will see that there are some capital costs, but these are mostly refundable in the long-term. Beyond these items, you are looking at a few thousand dollars for equipment, rent (if you decide to have an office), and the typical consumable items that any business uses on a day-to-day basis. Also, you need a good credit rating, since you will be entrusted with bail bonds worth hundreds of thousands of dollars, and you will be involved in holding collateral that belongs to other people.

Role in the Criminal Justice System

Are you a felon? If so, you should probably stop right here. Most states have rules prohibiting felons from becoming bail agents. Secondly, since you have access to the jails, the local Corrections Department will probably do some kind of a background check on you before providing a jail ID card. If you are a felon, you will be denied access to the jail.

Over time, you will become a very important cog in the criminal justice system. As such, you will receive calls from defendants, family members, lawyers, court clerks, and even an occasional call from a judge.

As I said in the Introduction, I went from being a Wall Street Stockbroker to being the local bail bondsman. My interaction with my customers was different in the two professions: as a Stockbroker, I heartily greeted my customers on the street; as a bail bondsman, I waited for my customers to greet me, so that I would not embarrass them in front of friends or family who did not know that they had been arrested.

You must understand that you will be providing bail for not only the lower economic classes, but also the affluent. In my mind, I carry a list of politicians, celebrities, and corporate leaders who have called me for bail.

Obligations of the Bail Agent

Simply stated, a bail agent has only three obligations:

1. Guarantee Appearance. Your job is to carefully underwrite any bail undertaking, and guarantee to the court that your defendant will appear.
2. Produce the Defendant. When the mail brings you a notice of failure to appear, it is your job to locate,

apprehend, and surrender the defendant back into the custody of law enforcement.

3. Pay the Bail. When you are unable to apprehend the defendant, you should pay the forfeited bail in a timely manner.

In these three statements, the complete job of a bail agent is summarized. If you adhere to these three statements, you will become a well-respected member of the criminal justice system.

How the Industry Is Organized

Surety Agents and Property Bondsmen

This is where we begin to truly understand how this business works. If you understand the way that the business is organized, you will be able to make some important decisions about whether you want to be a Property Bondsman (if allowed in your state) or a Surety Agent.

Although most bail agents write for surety insurance companies, many states still allow property bondsmen who write bail using their own assets as collateral with the state. In other words, rather than having a guarantee from an insurance company that backs the bail bond that you write, a property bondsman posts certain types of allowable collateral with the state as a guarantee that a defaulted bail will be paid. In many cases, the amount of bail that a property bondsman can write is a certain multiple of the amount of collateral on deposit with the state.

Here are a couple of examples:

1. In Alabama, you can write bail by posting $25,000 cash with the state for every county in which you do business. Statewide, this can require a large sum of money, but if you limit your activities to one or two counties, it can be the best route.

2. In Colorado, a Property Bondsman must have at least two years of experience to qualify. You must post

$50,000 with the state, but you can do business in any county.

3. In Texas and Georgia, Property Bondsmen are quite prevalent, but the requirements may vary from county to county. Check the local requirements.

4. Many other states (Arkansas, New Mexico, etc.) allow Property Bondsmen. Check with your state regulator for requirements.

What is the financial reason to be a property bondsman rather than a surety bail agent? If you write bail based upon your own assets, you do not have to share your revenues with anyone. Using a surety insurance company, you must pay bond costs and build-up funds as explained in the next section.

A property bondsman is totally on his own. There is no large entity with deep pockets available to assist if financial disaster should strike. Secondly, there may be a limit to the amount of business you can write due to the limited amount of collateral that you have on deposit with the state.

Before deciding on which road you want to take (property or surety), give some reflection to the Colorado rule which requires a property bondsman to have at least two years of experience.

Surety Insurance Company

A typical *casualty* insurance company may sell homeowners, business, or automobile insurance. The company expects to incur losses due to fire, theft, accident, etc., and has made provision within its premium rates for those payouts.

A *surety* insurance company, on the other hand, expects to have minimal losses, and will only write bonds guaranteeing something if there is an indemnitor, someone who guarantees against losses. From the company's point of view, a surety bail agent is the indemnitor for all of the bail bonds that he writes. As a result, the premium rate charged to the agent is less, but the contract will usually call for a build-up fund as described in the following section.

Contract With Surety Company

A typical contract with a surety insurance company has many provisions, written by lawyers for lawyers. However, in any contract, there are some provisions that you need to focus upon as the agent:

> 1. **Initial Collateral** is an initial deposit with the surety company to offset any potentials losses that you may incur for the company. This initial collateral could be in the range of $10,000 cash, a mortgage on a piece of real estate with lots of equity, etc. If the deposit is cash, the money is treated as a deposit into your Build-Up Fund, as defined below.

2. **Bond Cost** is the amount of premium that you will pay to the surety company for the privilege of using their bonds in your bail bond business. If you are new to the business, you can expect to be required to pay as much as 20% of your revenues to the company, because you do not have any track record for the company to measure your performance. Once you have a track record, you can expect to pay somewhere between 9% and 15% as Bond Cost.

3. **Build-Up Fund** is a continually growing cash fund held by the surety company, and used to pay any losses to the surety company that you may incur. The industry-wide standard for mandatory Build-Up Fund contributions is 10% of your revenues, although one company has been accepting rates as low as 5% if you are an experienced bail agent. Many agents try to use the assets of their Build-Up Funds to pay on-going bail forfeitures caused by FTA's. The intent of the fund is to protect the surety company and create a long-term savings account for the agent. If you change sureties or retire, this ever-growing amount of cash will be returned to you *when all of your bonds have been discharged with no losses to the surety company.*

4. **Underwriting Authority** limits your ability to validly write a bail bond above certain levels. Typically, an agent is initially limited to writing bonds of no more than

$10,000 or $25,000 without surety company approval. As you become more experienced, your underwriting authority will rise.

5. **Personal Liability** is the cornerstone of every surety insurance company contract. You will find a clause in the contract that says, no matter what happens, you are personally responsible for any losses to the company. My very first surety company also required that my spouse had to sign, assuming personal responsibility. You must be comfortable with risk, and be able to sleep at night knowing that you might be risking everything that you own on one or two large bails.

6. **Limitations set by the surety company** may also include a prohibition on writing bonds for any federal court. A bail bond in a state court typically guarantees only appearance, while a bail bond in many federal courts also guarantees performance. In other words, if a condition of bail is that a defendant cannot use any illegal drugs, and he fails a drug test, his bail bond can be forfeited even though he made every single court appearance.

Where To Find A Surety Company

Because bail is a niche market within the insurance industry, there are only about twenty-five companies, out of the thousands of insurance companies, which issue bail bonds. This small number fluctuates as companies enter and leave the business, but it seems to average around twenty-five.

Bail people who know the business well have started most bail surety insurance companies. The companies are either totally focused on bail, or have diversified slightly from bail. However, you should expect that any surety insurance company that you deal with is highly focused on the bail business.

Where can you find a surety insurance company? Because the companies tend to be smaller relative to State Farm or Liberty Mutual, many of them are not licensed in all fifty states and are regionally focused. You probably have never even heard of most of them.

In the chapter **A Short List of Surety Insurance Companies**, I give a list with names and contact information of companies that I feel comfortable recommending. Since bail is such a small and niche business, I personally know the people and companies that I have suggested that you contact.

Finally, the web site of the Professional Bail Agents of the United States (PBUS) provides a short list of companies that have purchased advertisements or supported the organization. Visit www.pbus.com to see that list.

Managing General Agent

Many surety insurance companies deal with their agents only through Managing General Agents (MGA's). For a national company, these MGA's are usually regionally based and are very well acquainted with the agents and markets that they supervise. The MGA's provide another level of financial security and safety for the surety company, in that the MGA's accept the financial responsibility for the agents that they put into the business.

For someone new to the business, or without deep pockets, working with an MGA can be very helpful. The MGA will provide advice, guidance, and sometimes a loan to pay that big forfeiture.

The disadvantage of working with an MGA is that your bond cost *may* be a little higher, since the MGA also needs to make money. However, the assistance provided may be well worth the additional bond cost.

General Agent

With most surety companies, the term General Agent is easy to define: the owner of the bail bond agency is the general agent. Some companies want to split hairs over this definition, but what *you* want to be is a General Agent, owner of the bail bond agency.

Along with the title come some disadvantages: you are the person who has signed the contract and you are liable for every bond that your or your sub-agents write. But it does mean that you are "The Boss".

Sub-Agent

A sub-agent is essentially your employee who holds a bail bond license. This person works for you and writes bonds at the jail, but has no liability for any losses. Typically, the General Agent has approved every bond that the sub-agent writes. After a period of time, the General Agent may give limited underwriting authority to the sub-agent.

If you start off as an individual bail agent, on call twenty-four hours a day, you will soon find that you need sub-agents in order to have any type of a personal life.

There are many ways that a sub-agent can be compensated: salary, hourly, commission, posting fee, etc. You should inquire as to what is common in your area since you do want to be competitive with the other bail agencies or your sub-agent will leave you.

Direct Writer

A Direct Writer is a General Agent who does not work through a Managing General Agent. The Direct Writer writes bail "directly" for the company, without the supervision or assistance of an MGA.

The advantage of being a Direct Writer is, of course, that your bond cost *may* be slightly lower. The disadvantage is that you have no local advisor.

Liable Versus Non-Liable Agents

During the past eight or ten years, some MGA's and surety companies experimented with issuing contracts in which the General Agent was not liable for any FTA's, but received a much smaller piece of the bail bond fee. Bond costs were in the 30% to 60% range, with no build-up funds.

From the agent's point of view, this sounds pretty good. All you have to do is give up a little bit larger piece of the fee, and you have no further responsibility for the bail bond once it has been written.

From the company's point of view, the strategy was disastrous. General Agents would bail essentially anyone, without regard for whether or not they expected the defendant to appear in court.

There are a few of these contracts still available in the marketplace. However, "there is no free lunch" in the business. If reckless underwriting drives your surety company into bankruptcy, the courts may still hold you responsible for the bail bonds that you wrote.

Bail Statutes in Your State

Review Your State's Statutes

Among the very first tasks that you should undertake to start your bail bond business is to review the statutes in your state. Usually, you will be able to find the statutes through the State web site using a keyword search.

Each state's statutes are different. States that have large bail markets (Florida, Texas, California, etc.) tend to have pages and pages of statute covering everything from a mandated office to types of advertising.

Smaller markets tend to have much less legislation. I have seen states in which the sum total of the legislation is a single paragraph that merely authorizes the existence of professional bail agents.

By reading through all of the applicable statutes, you will get a sense of the legislative attitude towards bail agents. Be sure to read all of the statutes, including those that are only mentioned by reference number to some other section of the law.

You must also check any administrative regulations issued by the regulating department. For example, in a surety only state, it is common for the State Department of Insurance (DOI) to be named as regulator.

Typically, the DOI will issue a plethora of regulations affecting everything from mileage reimbursement to solicitation in jails or courts.

The following subjects are some of the essential elements that you should review.

Requirements For Licensing

Licensing requirements are the first and foremost issues that you should review. If you cannot meet the licensing requirements at the first reading of the statute, is there any real basis to continue?

Regulations By Regulating Department

The regulating department (for example, the DOI) has probably issued a list of regulations that require your review. Again, the simple question is, if you cannot meet the licensing regulations at the first reading of the regulations, is there any real basis to continue?

Rules for Forfeiting Bail

Here we start reviewing some of the more interesting statutes and regulations. On what basis can bail be forfeited?

Your initial reaction may be that bail should only be forfeited if the defendant fails to appear in court. That, of course, is the ideal situation. However, reality is never ideal.

Some states and jurisdictions have "performance" standards written into their bail statutes. What this means is that the *bail bond that you post could be forfeited if the defendant violates a condition of his release other than failing to appear.*

In most cases, a defendant must sign a "terms of release" document that stipulates such things as no illegal drug use, no alcohol, no further arrest, etc. If the defendant is arrested for some other crime, the court *may* forfeit bail because of the violation of conditions.

Read the statutes very closely, and then inquire as to common practice in the courts about forfeiture. Many (if not most) courts usually ignore the performance standards for forfeiture. A good source for information will be your district or superior court clerk.

Basis to Vacate Forfeiture

Typically, you would vacate a forfeiture of bail by apprehending the defendant, surrendering him to local law enforcement, and submitting a motion to the court to vacate the forfeiture. However, you must be aware of time limits.

Does your state have a time limit on remission (vacating a forfeiture)? Some states have as few as thirty days, while other states have six months. In other words, you may be required to produce the defendant within thirty days, or pay the forfeited bail at that point.

Does your state allow remission after the payment of the forfeited bail? Some states have a strict limitation of two years on final remission, while other states allow court discretion in this matter.

The other aspect of remission that you should search the statutes for is the technical standards for the judge or clerk to forfeit the bail. In other words, if proper notice is not sent within the specified period of time, are you discharged from the bail? What happens if the defendant is deceased, or is incarcerated in another state?

Vacating a forfeiture is much more complicated that just apprehending a defendant, particularly when you cannot produce the defendant for some technical reason. You need to understand the statutes of your state in this matter.

Licensing

Regulation of the Business

Having familiarized yourself with the state statutes regarding bail and bail agents, you now know which state, county or local department regulates the profession. Call ahead and set up an appointment with the head of the department that regulates bail agents.

This might seem like an unlikely step, but it will benefit you in many ways. First, the person within the department will get to meet you face-to-face and know you as a human being. Secondly, this regulator can explain the most difficult aspects of licensing and how to overcome them. Thirdly, this person will have a unique view of the business---with a discrete inquiry, you might be able to find out who is retiring and looking for a buyer of his business. This appointment is a great opportunity to learn otherwise unavailable information.

When I began the process of getting licensed, I met with the regulator to discuss the many steps of licensing. The statutory requirement was that I have a property and casualty insurance license, which I did. However, I also learned that there was a separate bail agent's exam that was administered by the regulator, who was able to tell me what material I should be studying.

Never underestimate the power of personal interaction!

Before moving on to another subject, I do want to mention that Florida has established an internship period, which has also been proposed in some other states. The basic requirement is that a new licensee must work for an experienced bail agent for a stipulated period of time before establishing an independent agency.

This internship requirement is justified by the need to "learn" the business, in the same way that apprentices and interns in other businesses are required to learn over time from experienced licensees.

The internship is understandable, but it does provide an obstacle to entry into the business. A new licensee may have to intern for up to a year before establishing his own agency. Check you state's statute for any mention of this provision.

Fidelity Bond

A few states require a fidelity bond before you can receive your license. A typical fidelity bond is set in the amount of $10,000, and will cost you anywhere from $100 to $250 per year.

Sometimes referred to as an "honesty" bond, this is designed to protect the public in the event that you abscond with customer monies. Many insurance agencies that deal with fidelity bonds have never issued a bond for a bail agent. The agencies may find that their regular insurance company will refuse a bail agent. If you have trouble finding an honesty bond, please check the list of **Miscellaneous Contacts** in the Appendix for the information of the insurance agency in Indiana that I use.

Appointment by Sheriff for Property Bondsmen

In some states, property bondsmen are appointed through the local sheriff. There are some areas where the sheriff limits appointments to only two bondsmen in the county in order to maintain close supervision. If this is the situation in your area, you may find yourself locked out of the business by the limitation on bondmen. Essentially, there is nothing that you can do about this situation. Check the surety agent situation to see if you can qualify by representing a surety insurance company.

Cash deposits and posting limitations are typically set by statute. In most cases, the cash deposits are held directly by the courts or through the State Treasurer's office.

Appointment by Insurance Department

A bail agent representing a surety insurance company is most often appointed through the State Department of Insurance. The appointment is usually contingent upon the applicant having the appropriate insurance license in that state.

Many states require that a bail agent have a property and casualty insurance license. Frankly, this is one of the hardest licenses to get due to the difficulty of the material and the state's licensing examination. If your state requires that you have a property and casualty license, and you do not already have it, I suggest that you do one of the week-long study courses that are usually offered through insurance schools or the Professional Insurance Agents Association www.pianet.com. .

Other states have what is called a "limited lines license". It is an insurance license limited to a certain type of insurance, such as bail bonds. If your state has a "limited lines license", you are fortunate because you will not have to learn about homeowners, automobile, or inland marine insurance. (I have always thought of inland marine as oxymoronic).

Once you have the license and have signed a contract with a surety insurance company, you will receive a Power of Attorney (POA) from the company to give to the regulator. The POA is official notice to the state or local regulator that you are authorized to write bail bonds on behalf of that surety company. In the Appendix, you will find an example of an actual POA.

Bail Enforcement Agent (Bounty Hunter)

During your review of bail statutes, you should have found references to bail enforcement agents, bail recovery agents, bounty hunters, private investigators, etc. The popularized name for these people is, of course, bounty hunters.

- 37 -

When you receive notice of an FTA, you will want to be able to dispatch a Bail Enforcement Agent (BEA) to apprehend the fugitive, or you may want to do it yourself. As your business grows, you will find that you do not have the time to spend on the streets looking for fugitives.

Although many states have no statute requiring licensing or other limitations on BEA's, it is becoming more and more common to see statute and regulations being implemented. At the website of the California Bail Agents Association www.cbaa.com, you will find the California Bail Recovery Agent statute, which is a good example of legislation on this subject.

Other states have dealt with the issue by legislating that only licensed bail agents can make apprehensions (Florida), or that only a licensed Private Investigator may apprehend a fugitive (Texas, Arkansas). Again, you need to carefully review your state's statutes to determine if and how a BEA is regulated.

Understanding the Bail Markets

Size of Statewide Markets

What is the size of the opportunity to write bail in your state? The extremes are probably California (estimated at up to $2 *billion*) and Vermont (estimated at $1.5 *million*) in penal amount of bonds written. If you accept the premise (arguable) that the typical bail bond fee is 10% of the bail, then revenues to the California market are $200,000,000 and revenues to the Vermont market are $150,000.

Which market would you rather be in?

The source of information for your market will be the local regulator. When you meet with him, ask for an estimate of the total penal amount of bail written in the state, the number of agencies and the number of licensees. By taking ten percent of the statewide penal amount and dividing it by the number of agencies, you can determine how much revenue *on average* each agency is taking from the market.

Regardless of your own expectations, in the first couple of years of your business, you will not do as much as an average agency. However, the average revenue number will give you a feel for how the business is going in your state.

Will you be financially successful if you are an average agency? Setting aside all other feelings about bail, this might be the point at which you decide that there really is not enough revenue in the market to attain your personal financial objective.

Remember, in any business you must maintain financial objectivity. If the market is too small, or the competition is too fierce, you may decide to look elsewhere for your financial success.

Most Competitive Markets

The states with the largest bail revenues are also typically the most competitive markets. For examples of this, you can look at California, Texas, Florida, Oklahoma, etc. There is a lot of bail written in these states, which means that there are a lot of bail agents.

Open your local *Yellow Pages* and look under the heading "Bail Bonds". Count the number of bail bond agencies that are listed there, and carefully examine the display advertisements. If you tell me that there are only four or five names listed, with small block advertisements, I would be very interested. If you tell me that there are two or three dozen listings, with full-page or double-page advertisements, I would say that you are in a very competitive market.

You need to carefully assess the market and the competition. Bail agencies can be very cutthroat in pursuit of writing bail.

"No Bail" States

As of this writing, there are four states that are referred to as "no bail" states --- Oregon, Illinois, Kentucky and Wisconsin. If you are thinking about starting a business in those states, it will not be possible. However, you do need to keep your eye on legislation in those states, because there are repeated attempts to bring bail back. If you live in those states, be ready to capitalize on legislative change.

In addition to states where legislation was passed to remove bail-bonding opportunities, there are a few states that strongly discourage it and will not license you.

For a number of years, I tried to get licensed in Massachusetts. There is currently only one bail agent licensed in a state with millions of people and large amounts of crime. The state regulator has refused to grant any more licenses, even though I sued him in federal and state court.

In Maine, there are no bail agents, even though the statutes allow for bail bonding. I took a different approach in Maine by hiring a respected lobbyist to talk with the judges about bail. The court system responded that they did not want bail agents or bail enforcement agents working in the state.

As you can see, even if there are laws allowing bail agents, you may not have the opportunity to start your business, Check the local environment very carefully!

Federal Bonds

As was mentioned earlier, many federal courts will forfeit bail not only for failure to appear, but also for violation of conditions. As a result, many surety companies print on their bail bonds "Not Valid In Federal Courts".

There are always exceptions to the rule. For example, the federal courts in Southern Florida accept bail bonds on an appearance basis only. Secondly, the Professional Bail Agents of the United States (PBUS) have made repeated attempts to limit federal forfeiture to failure to appear. You must review the federal situation in your area to assess whether you can write bail for the federal courts.

If you find that there is opportunity in your federal court district, call the federal Clerk of Court to make an appointment to introduce yourself. You will find that federal courts will accept bonds from any bail agent who has been properly licensed by the state.

- 42 -

Terminology

Every business has its own vocabulary or jargon, and bail is no different. In this chapter, I have listed all of the common terms that are used, and I have provided some explanation. In order to interact with customers, jail personnel, court staff, etc., you need to understand the language. Secondly, the explanations of the jargon will help you to understand many aspects of the business.

Defendant or Principal

In criminal justice terms, the defendant is the individual accused of a crime. The defendant was arrested, booked and arraigned on a charge or allegation made by the arresting authority.

In insurance terms, the defendant is also known as the principal. The surety or bail bond is guaranteeing that the defendant/principal will do some stated act, namely appearing in court for all of his hearings.

You will often see the defendant referred to as the principal when a court is rendering a decision concerning a bail bond because at that point the court is discussing insurance matters. Here again is part of the quote from the case of Taylor v. Taintor: *". . . The bail have their principal on a string, and may pull the string whenever they please, and render him in their discharge . . ."*

Obligor

The obligor is an insurance term for the person (property bondsman or surety insurance company) who is issuing a bond to guarantee the performance of the defendant. The obligor is obligated to pay the court in the event that the defendant fails to perform his duty to appear in court.

Obligee

The obligee is the person to whom a bond is given, meaning the court in the case of the bail bond process. In other words, the obligee is the entity that is paid if the principal fails to perform, as guaranteed by the obligor.

Surety

The surety is both a legal and an insurance term for someone or something that guarantees the performance of the principal/defendant. In bail bond terms, the surety is the bail agent and the surety insurance company.

Indemnitor

An indemnitor guarantees or indemnifies someone against loss. An indemnitor may sign a promissory note or put up collateral to indemnify the bail agent against any loss from posting a bail bond. Typically, an indemnitor is an employer, parent or other family member.

Underwriting Guidelines

These are a set of rules that a bail agent may use to decide whether or not to post a bail band for a defendant. The initial underwriting guidelines are limitations set by a surety insurance company that require the bail agent to get approval for bails over a certain amount – (i.e.) $10,000. $25,000, or $50,000.

Bail Bond Fee

The bail bond fee is the amount of money paid to the bail agent by the indemnitor to post the bond. The fee is usually set by state law, is not refundable, and averages 10% of the bail.

Collateral

Collateral is something of value that is given to the bail agent by the indemnitor to guarantee the bail agent against loss. The collateral is most often a sum of money, mortgage to real estate, or some other easily liquidated asset that the bail agent holds until the defendant's case has concluded. As long as the defendant appears at all of his court dates, the collateral is fully refundable to the indemnitor.

Bond Cost

A surety bail agent representing a surety insurance company must pay that company a fee for each bond written. Referred to as bond cost, the fee runs 9% to 20% of the bail bond fee.

Build-Up Fund (BUF)

A surety insurance company typically requires that a bail agent must make a continuing deposit of cash into a Build-Up Fund with the company that is used to safeguard the company against losses from bonds that the agent has written. Most Build-Up Fund requirements are 10% of the bail bond fee, but lower rates can be negotiated with the company.

Cash Only Bail

Cash only bail is usually only set when a judge wants to make it extremely difficult for a defendant to get out of jail. A bail agent's bond will not be accepted. Only cash can be presented to provide bail. Some states do not allow cash only bail, but most still give the judge the discretion to use this type of bail.

Cash or Surety Bail

Cash or surety bail is the typical secured bail used by most courts. It simply means that the family may post cash directly to bail a defendant, or that a bail agent's bond (surety) can be posted.

Personal Recognizance

Personal recognizance is unsecured bail, meaning that no cash or bond is posted to allow the defendant to be released. The defendant merely signs a promise to appear in court for all of his court dates.

Credit Bonding and Time Payments

Credit bonding and time payments allow an indemnitor to pay the bail bond fee over time, rather than a full amount upfront. Some states have made this unlawful, while others frown upon the practice.

Jails versus Prisons

A jail is usually run by the city or county, and is designed for pre-trial custody and short sentences (less than a year). A prison is run by the state and holds inmates who have been sentenced to at least one year and as long as life in prison.

Forfeiture

When a defendant fails to appear in court as ordered, the judge will forfeit the bail, which means that a bail agent will receive a notice to produce the defendant within a specified period of time or pay the bail.

Revocation

Revocation of bail is an action by the bail agent or surety to surrender the defendant to the court and have all further obligation discharged.

Remission

Remission is an action of the court to vacate the forfeiture of bail after the forfeiture has been paid. Most states have specific periods of remission, which might be two years.

Bail Enforcement Agent

Popularly referred to as bounty hunters, bail enforcement agents are authorized by bail agents to apprehend fugitives. In some states, licensing and insurance is required.

Discharge or Exoneration

When a criminal case is concluded, the court will send a discharge or exoneration, which is the official notice that the bail agent's liability is over.

Appearance versus Performance Bond

Most bail bonds merely guarantee that a defendant will appear in court as ordered. However, in some jurisdictions and most federal courts, a bail bond also guarantees that the defendant will adhere to the conditions of his bail, such as not drinking. Thus, the bond guarantees that the defendant will perform to the standard of the court by not drinking.

Posting Fee

A bail agent may post a bond at the request of his surety insurance company, because another bail agent has guaranteed the bond. The bail agent posting the bond will be paid a posting fee for his services.

Women in Bail

Many Women Own Bail Agencies

If you take my advice and go to the conventions of PBUS (www.pbus.com) or the state associations, you will meet many women who are in the bail bond business. And they are making good money doing it!

At one of my first PBUS conventions, I met a rather elderly woman, in her eighties, who was confined to an electric wheel chair. She was the owner of one of the biggest bail agencies in California. Let me tell you her story.

In the early 1960's, this lovely lady owned a hairdressing salon. One night, she was awakened by a telephone call from an employee who needed to be bailed from jail. How to do it? She looked in the *Yellow Pages* and called a bail bondsman, who met her at the jail and accepted a hefty fee to bail the employee.

It was two weeks later that she received a telephone call from *another* employee who also needed bail. The process was repeated, and again she paid a hefty fee to the bail bondsman.

Well, you did not have to hit this lady on the head with a baseball bat to make her realize that something profitable was going on here.

There was a very small storefront next to her salon that was vacant, and in a couple of months she was in the bail bond business.

14,000 Agents in US, 48% are Women

The Professional Bail Agents of the United States estimate that there are 14,000 licensed bail agents in the country, and that 48% of them are women. Women are so common in the bail bond business that PBUS has a special workshop at each of their conventions titled "For Women Only". It is the best-attended workshop at the convention, but I have not attended because I am a man.

The bail bond business is made up of entrepreneurs, both women and men. Presidents of PBUS and the state associations are commonly women who are highly regarded by their colleagues.

Are Women Better Than Men?

In my mind, the answer to this question is a very loud, "Yes!" Among my employees, the women bail agents have always had fewer FTA's than the men. I believe that the so-called "sixth sense" among women works very well in bail.

Is It Safe?

The bail bond business is as safe as you make it. I have never felt threatened or endangered in any way. I believe that my women agents would tell you the very same thing.

Among bail recovery agents, there is a high percentage of women, usually working with a team of men. My interest, and the interest of this book, is how to make money running a bail bond agency, rather than being a bail recovery agent.

Establishing Your Bail Bond Business

Is Bail Viable In Your Area?

Before spending any money or signing surety insurance company contracts, you need to be convinced that a new bail bond business is viable in your area. In other words, you have to determine the profitability of the various bail agencies in your area and determine whether or not you can get a reasonable piece of the overall business.

In my own experience starting my bail bond business, I determined that there was plenty of room for another bail agency, and that my competitors' weakest points were in the area of customer service: no toll-free numbers, not accepting collect calls, not going out in the middle of the night, etc.

This really goes back to the discussion in the chapter **Understanding the Bail Markets**; if you truly understand your local situation, you can make a proper assessment of your potential success.

To Buy or to Start New?

The question of whether to buy an on-going business or to start a new one is really based upon the business offered for purchase. Is it one of the major bail bond businesses in the area? Does it have a good cash flow?

What do the tax returns tell you about the profitability? Tax returns will be your key documents, determining whether the owners have actually reported and paid taxes on their income. (See the chapter **Day to Day Business Operations** for an extensive discussion of taxes).

If your market is made up mostly of small bail bond businesses operated as a part-time or sideline business, it is probably best to start a new business. You will be able to compete with the part-timers, and capture business using the techniques in the **Advertising and Promotion** chapter. But, if your market is very competitive, buying an on-going business has many advantages, including the following:

1. An immediate cash flow, from the time that you take over the business.

2. Trained and experienced employees, who can help you to learn the business.

3. An established presence in the market, including telephone numbers, offices, and extensive base of satisfied and repeat customers, etc.

4. The list of benefits from buying an on-going business can be quite long, so do some reading about it.

One word of caution regarding the purchase of an on-going business: there may be many hidden liabilities that you do not want to assume. Be sure to carefully review the transaction with your attorney and your certified public accountant. Many people discuss the transaction with

- 54 -

their attorney, but do not include one person who can help you dramatically, the CPA.

Naming Your Business

Yes, the proper naming of your bail bond business will result in more calls and more bails. Here are a few personal rules that I developed for myself about business names:

1. Make sure the name tells people what you do; include the words "bail bonds" in the name. The name might be "AAA Bail Bonds, Inc."

2. Try not to confuse people with technical terms in your name. "AAA Surety, Inc." is not as effective as "AAA Bail Bonds, Inc."

3. Do not name the business after yourself, such as "Doestoevsky Bail Bonds, Inc." First, people cannot pronounce your name properly (as is my case), and, second, when you sell the business, you might not want your name associated with the new owners.

4. Yes, unfortunately, potential bail bond customers refer to the *Yellow Pages* and start calling from the top of the list. Realize that you want your business at or near the top of the list, so name the business appropriately. Talk to a *Yellow Pages* consultant about this.

Corporation or Sole Proprietorship

It is usually to your advantage to run your business through a corporation, "S" corporation or limited liability corporation. You need to discuss this at length with your attorney or CPA.

The benefit of any of the corporate structures usually is in the liability area. The corporate veil will help to protect your other assets. Remember, though, that you are and will be *personally* liable for all of the bail bonds that your business writes. Again, this is an area that needs thorough examination by your attorney.

Insurance

If you are in the bail bond business, insurance is hard to get, particularly liability insurance.

A few years ago, the Professional Bail Agents of the United States were able to put together a general liability insurance program, but the insurer cancelled the program after a few years do to poor experience. The question of liability insurance remains high on the PBUS agenda, so stay connected to the association so that you know the situation.

An Office versus a Telephone Number?

What do I mean by asking this question, "An office or a telephone number?"

Doesn't everybody have an office? Obviously, the answer is No! During my whole career as a bail agent, running a statewide and multi-state organization, I never had a formal office. My office was in the attic of my home.

As I have explained previously, my market was small, semi-rural, and required extensive travel across the state to the county jails. The competitive situation was that no one had offices, just *Yellow Pages* listings with telephone numbers that were forwarded out to cell phones. I answered the calls for bail as I traveled from jail to jail.

Again, you must know your market. Is it just one huge jail downtown? Do the other agencies have large, storefront offices with flashing neon signs? If so, you will probably have to take the plunge by opening an office and incurring that monthly expense.

Getting Your Name Posted At the Jail

In most markets, getting your name posted at the jail is usually just a formality after the regulatory authority has licensed you. Most jails do not want to be accused of favoritism, so a complete list is posted in alphabetical order. Refer to the section **Naming Your Business** to understand how to capitalize on this.

Accepting collect calls and using a toll-free telephone number are necessities for getting the most number of calls from the jail. In the chapter **Advertising and Promotion**, this subject will be explored fully.

In a very few jurisdictions, the courts or statutes have mandated the installation of direct lines from the jail to bail bond offices. When a defendant picks up the handset, the line starts to ring in the bail bond office. If you are in one of these few jurisdictions, be sure that the direct line is installed immediately.

Equipment

Unlike a restaurant or construction business, a bail bond office needs very little equipment beyond a file cabinet and a computer, which are ubiquitous today. However, as your business grows, you will need software and perhaps an office network to keep track of your defendants, do discharge reports, accounting, etc. If you are going to buy a new computer get something with a high-speed processor and a large amount of memory (particularly if you are going to be taking digital pictures of your defendants, as explained in following sections).

Become a Credit Card Merchant

Acceptance of credit cards is an absolute necessity. There are many bail agents who do not accept credit cards, for reasons including cost of processing fees, difficulty, preference for cash, etc. If you accept credit cards, you will have a significant advantage over your competitors.

Be sure to put the various credit card logos in all of your advertising, particularly the *Yellow Pages*.

Over the years, I could not count how many times I have received a telephone call from hundreds or thousands of miles away from a parent or employer trying to bail some defendant in my state. My strategy was very simple: I would put the whole amount of the bail, plus my fee, on a credit card. This created a risk-free situation, so that someone from far away could arrange bail. In almost every single instance, the caller would immediately begin reading the number from his credit card!

Credit card processing companies do not like the bail bond business. Apparently, the companies have had bad experiences in the bail business, and have globally rejected most bail agents.

If you have a good working relationship with your local bank, you might be able to become a credit card merchant with them, or you may be surprised when they are required by the processing company to terminate you.

How can you become a credit card merchant?

For many years, one credit card processor, American Spirit Processing, Inc. www.americanspiritprocessing.com has welcomed the bail bond business. The company's President, James Peeler, email sales@americanspiritprocessing.com, is a regular vendor at the PBUS and state association meetings. Mr. Peeler can provide you with processing when no one else will!

If you mention this book as your source of information for the processing, the company will give you a discount on the regular rates charged.

Check Guarantee Service

Perhaps a third of your customers will offer you a personal check for the bail bond fee and/or collateral. Very few bail agents accept checks for fear that they are made from rubber!

If you use a check guarantee service and prominently advertise "Personal Checks Accepted", particularly in the *Yellow Pages*, you will substantially increase your business. However, like credit cards, the check guarantee business has had a poor experience with bail agents.

Once again, American Spirit Processing, Inc. www.americanspiritprocessing.com and James Peeler have provided the bail bond community with a service that no one else can provide. They can provide you with a check guarantee service that works for the bail bond business. Contact Mr. Peeler at sales@americanspiritprocessing.com.

Again, if you mention this book as your source of information for the processing, the company will give you a discount on the regular rates charged.

Your Business Briefcase

Forms

As mentioned earlier, I carried a large, catalogue style briefcase to hold all of the forms and equipment that I needed to do a bail. Here is a brief list and explanation of the forms (available in the **Forms** chapter of this book) that I always carried with me:

1. Application Form - The basic application form is the most essential document of any bail. The form will collect information on both the defendant and the Indemnitor, and includes a necessary promissory note from the Indemnitor. In the event of an FTA, this application form will have all of the information that you need to give to the bail enforcement agent.

2. Mortgage Form - As a standard underwriting guideline, I always used real estate or a significant amount of cash as the collateral for a bail over $10,000. Although I have included in the **Forms** chapter the type of mortgage form that I used in my area, you should have your attorney draft a document for you, and explain how to record it at the registry of deeds.

3. Bonds and Receipts – If you are a surety agent, you will have bonds and receipts for payment and collateral, as supplied by the surety insurance company. Usually, these are numbered forms with three parts: bond, payment receipt, and collateral receipt. Each item has the same number and requires the signature of the agent and the Indemnitor. When you have sub-agents working for you, the numbered receipts allow you to track bonds, payments and collateral.

4. Bail Recovery Agent Contracts – You should be prepared at any time to dispatch your bail enforcement agent for a fugitive apprehension. Time can often mean a significant amount of money!

5. Business Cards – Carry lots of business cards with you. I made a habit of giving every Indemnitor and every defendant two cards, saying, "Here's one card for your wallet and one card for you to give to a friend."

Camera

Part of your routine for posting a bond must be taking the defendant's picture. In the event of an FTA, your bail enforcement agent will need a good photograph of the fugitive.

Many bail agents have begun using digital cameras, transferring the photo to their computer electronically. A digital camera is fine until you have a number of sub-agents working for you. Some of these sub-agents will be doing many bails, while others will be doing just a few. Slowly but surely, pictures get confused or lost simply do to volume.

As my business expanded, I returned to an instant (Polaroid) camera for each of my sub-agents. The picture of the defendant was taken at the jail and *immediately* stapled into the application form. In this way, there was no confusion or lost pictures.

Credit Card Machine and Charge Slips

I have previously stressed the importance of accepting credit cards. You need to carry a credit card machine and charge slips in your briefcase.

Many bail agents use a cellular style machine that allows you to swipe the card, enter the amount, and quickly get an authorization code. These machines are expensive and heavy.

I preferred to use a small slide-type machine to imprint a charge slip. Then I called the authorization center, where I entered the information through the keypad of my telephone.

Never agree to meet someone at the jail or elsewhere without first getting their credit card number and calling for an authorization. It is amazing how many times I heard the phrase, "Authorization Denied".

Miscellaneous

Check the **Giveaways** section of the **Advertising and Promotion** chapter for a list of all the things that I carried in my bag to give away as promotional items.

Eventually, you will find that your bag is loaded with many things that you feel are important. This is why I ended up carrying the catalogue style briefcase.

Steps in the Posting of a Bail Bond

Discuss Defendant with Indemnitor

Typically, the first contact that you will have with a bail is a telephone call from either the defendant or the Indemnitor. This is your opportunity to gather as much information as possible to see whether you will be willing to actually post a bail bond on behalf of the defendant. Secondly, you have the chance to learn about the Indemnitor and evaluate their credit worthiness and relationship to the defendant.

I always liked an indemnitor who was related to the defendant as parent or employer. In many cases, this initial call will come from a spouse who was the victim of domestic violence. Remember, a wife or children are always much more creditable as indemnitors than "fiancées" or "girlfriends". A fiancée today can quickly become a vindictive ex-fiancée next week, demanding that the defendant's bail be revoked.

Underwriting

At this point, you get to make a decision on whether to post the bond. Underwriting is an insurance term that is usually meant to express a level of investigation into the circumstances of a policy.

From a bail point of view, underwriting means searching for as much information about the defendant and indemnitor as possible, determining what (if any) collateral you would require to post the bond, and making that final decision to write the bail based upon your "gut" instinct.

Underwriting guidelines are usually self-imposed (or surety company imposed) rules to protect yourself from jumping at a large, but very risky, bail that might not be properly secured with collateral. As an example, you could use my rule that any bail over $10,000 had to be secured with real estate or a cash deposit.

What if you really do not want to do this bond? I always referred customers that I thought were bad risks to my biggest competitor. I wanted the customer to think that I was helping him, and I wanted my competitor to take the high flight risks.

In the following chapter, we will discuss underwriting rules at length.

Negotiate Fee and Collateral

A bail agent's fee is usually set by law, but in many states the fee can be negotiated to a lower level, or paid over time, which is the same thing as negotiating it to a lower level. A time payment is commonly referred to as "credit bonding", and, if not outlawed by the state, is frowned upon in many states. However, from a competitive point of view, if your market is doing time payments, you should expect that you would have to offer this service.

Collateral in the bail bond business is one of those terms that will sometimes defy definition. Obviously, collateral is used to secure the bond. If the defendant fails to appear, collateral can be used to offset the expenses of paying for his apprehension, or even to pay the final forfeiture due to the court.

But what is collateral? What can a bail agent use to secure a bail bond?

Probably, the most common type of collateral is the "signature bond". This is a bail bond that is guaranteed merely by the indemnitor's personal signature stating that he assumes all liability for financial losses if the defendant fails to appear in court. This type of bond is most common for amounts less than $10,000 where the indemnitor is an employer, parent, child, or spouse (particularly in a domestic violence case).

In larger bails, collateral can be defined as an automobile, a cash deposit, real estate, etc. Again, in the following chapter, we will discuss how to deal with the various types of collateral.

Meet Indemnitor, Receive Fee and Collateral

In most cases, you will meet the indemnitor at your office, or in a conference room at the jail. By meeting personally with the indemnitor, you have a further opportunity to assess the credit-worthiness of this person.

This is your opportunity to collect as much information as possible about the indemnitor. Ask to see his driver's license, copy all of the pertinent information including license number, get addresses and telephone numbers of employers, relatives, and friends.

You will be receiving your fee and the collateral that you negotiated. You must give separate receipts for the fee and the collateral. Once a defendant's case is discharged, you will be returning that collateral.

Are you taking real estate as collateral? This is when you will have the promissory note and mortgage signed and notarized.

Interview the Defendant at the Jail

Once you are done with the indemnitor, it is time to enter the jail and meet the defendant. Again, this is your opportunity to assess the risk level of this defendant, and gather as much information as possible.

Your questions will go far beyond name and address, to include probation officer, friends at alcoholics anonymous, drug counselors, etc. Do not be afraid to ask any question! Remember that this defendant will give you any information if it will help him to get out of jail.

Pictures of the defendant are an absolute necessity. Take two pictures to be sure that you have his appearance well documented. Your bail enforcement agent will greatly appreciate fairly close-up, in-focus pictures of the defendant.

Review both the defendant's and the indemnitor's portions of the application. Make sure that all of the blanks are completed, and that the signatures are there.

In some jurisdictions, it is not possible to interview the defendant at the jail. This creates a tricky situation in which you have to get the defendant to come to your office for questioning and pictures *after* he has been released.

Post the Bond at the Jail or Court

The actual posting of the bond can happen at the jail or at the courthouse.

The bail commissioner at the jail will usually receive the bond and instruct the jail to release the defendant. However, some jurisdictions require that the bond be posted at the court during court hours, and the clerk of court then instructs the jail to release the defendant.

Defendant Is Released

As a bail agent in a fairly rural state, I entered the jail and left with the defendant. However, in many states the jails are huge operations and the bureaucratic process to release a prisoner is quite lengthy. In some jurisdictions, it can take twelve to eighteen hours before the defendant is released.

From a customer service point of view, it is important to let your indemnitor know that the release is a lengthy process, so that he will not expect immediate results when you come out of the jail or courthouse. Being open and as informative as possible is the best marketing approach.

Day-to-Day Business Operations

Develop Clear Underwriting Guidelines

As mentioned earlier, you need to develop a set of clear underwriting guidelines, which you should carefully write out and review for yourself and your sub-agents. In the military, battle plans and other preparations are made before hostilities break out. In bail, you should follow the same philosophy of planning ahead, so that you do not write "bad bail" when you are called to quickly make a decision about a defendant.

Here is a list of the subjects that you should include in your underwriting guidelines:

1. Who qualifies for signature bonds? Under $10,000; never failed to appear; indemnitor is a homeowner or employer; not a high-risk crime involving drugs, sexual assault, etc. that means a long sentence.

2. Who qualifies for release without an indemnitor? Most domestic violence; local roots with parents, family, etc; credit card holder with a large credit limit; has a job and is a homeowner; low-risk crime.

3. Who needs partial cash collateral? A "real" crime such as burglary, robbery, stabbings, etc.; lack of a job and family roots; high-risk crime.

4. Who needs real estate collateral? Bails over $10,000; potentially a very long sentence to prison; high-risk crime.

Having said all of the above, I will admit that I have violated every underwriting rule that I have written. I have done signature bonds for $100,000, and I have released defendants on their own for $50,000. It is the old saying about every situation is different. However, as you start out in the bail bond business, you need to tread carefully and obey your own underwriting rules to avoid large problems early in your career.

Monitoring

You may want to monitor certain of your defendants much more closely than others. A high-risk defendant should be monitored in one form or another.

Monitoring can be done electronically (see the **Related Businesses** chapter) or it can be done through telephone calls, personal visits to your office, caller ID, telephone traps, etc. The PBUS conventions will be an excellent source for various techniques and equipment.

Accounting System

As a business owner, you have to have a good accounting system to meet the requirements of state and federal law, and provide a track record for anyone who might want to buy your business in the future. Good accounting software is a necessity, and is relatively cheap.

For years, I used *Quickbooks*, the accounting software developed and sold by Intuit Corporation www.intuit.com. There is no doubt that *Quickbooks* is the leader in accounting software, and has become the standard for small business.

When it comes to preparing the payroll, there is always the question of using a payroll service, or doing it yourself. Beyond the complexity of the process, there are certain business considerations.

I met at least weekly with each of my sub-agents in my office. After thoroughly reviewing each new defendant folder, I would calculate the sub-agent's earnings (my sub-agents were paid on commission, as a stimulus to get them out of bed in the middle of the night to do a bail). I found it best to enter the information into my *Quickbooks* system at that time, and immediately issue a paycheck to the sub-agent when he turned in the files.

Employees or Subcontractors?

Are your sub-agents and bail enforcement agents subcontractors or employees from the Internal Revenue Service's (IRS) point of view? The difference can be important, particularly as regards social security and Medicare taxes, along with withholding. Do you as an employer have to pay social security/Medicare taxes and deposit tax withholdings?

Both my lawyer and my accountant gave me a very solid answer. Yes, they are employees. The IRS has certain tests of employee/subcontractor status that involve behavioral, financial, and relationship tests. One of the very best explanations of this IRS test is located on the Texas Department of Labor's website at http://www.twc.state.tx.us/news/efte/appx_d_irs_ic_test.html.

Determining employee status is just one reason out of dozens to have a close relationship with a good accountant who can do both your business and personal tax returns. If you have established a corporation or partnership to own your business, the taxes get very complicated, very quickly.

According to the IRS audit guide for the bail bond business, two out of three bail bond businesses do not even file tax returns, never mind understate income or overstate expenses. This has made the bail bond business a high profile area for the IRS. To fully understand the many things that the IRS will look at, feel free to download the IRS audit guide from my website at www.howtostartabailbondbusiness.com.

Workers' Compensation Insurance is mandated for employees and subcontractors in every state. Although the rate per employee for bail bond agencies is relatively low, you might find that the cumulative premium adds to a good-sized bill. For the sake of your employees, and to avoid nasty fines and litigation, be sure to have a proper workers' compensation policy in place.

Financial Accounts and Cash Collateral

To properly manage your bail bond business, you will need two bank accounts, an Operating Account and a Collateral Account.

Since any cash collateral that you accept is really not yours, but belongs to the indemnitor, it must be segregated and accounted for through a separate bank account and in *Quickbooks*.

One of the things that can get your insurance/bail license revoked very quickly is the improper handling of collateral funds. You are subject to audit by both your surety insurance company and your state regulator. Handle other people's cash very carefully.

Of course, your operating account is used to meet your everyday income and expense needs. Your accounting software will be extremely helpful when tax time comes.

Non-Cash Collateral

I have been offered everything imaginable as collateral, from toolboxes full of tools to jewelry or "other services". In the end, I always liked cash or real estate.

You will be offered automobiles, motorcycles, jewelry, Rolex watches, and all kinds of other things as collateral. But what are they *really* worth if you had to sell them? And how will you store and safeguard this collateral? I would much rather have small amounts of cash as collateral than all of the automobile titles that you could give me. Who's going to pick up that automobile when the defendant flees driving the automobile that you have the title to? Cash and real estate make the best collateral.

Reporting Requirements

Even though you are your own boss, there are a couple of organizations that you are required to report to on a regular basis:

1. Your surety insurance company.
2. Your state regulator.

On at least a monthly basis, but probably on a weekly basis, you will need to report bonds executed and discharged to your surety insurance company. If you do not report regularly, you will quickly run out of bonds, as the company will only send bonds to replace those that have been reported as executed. Along with executions, you must report discharges, which will be discussed in the next section.

In many states, you are required to report at least monthly to the state regulator on all bonds posted, typically by county. Some states regard this information as public, while others regard it as confidential business/trade information.

If your state treats the information as public, this is a great source to gain insight into how well your competitors are doing relative to your business.

Importance of Bond Discharges

Bond discharges are the notices from a court that your defendant's case is over, and you no longer have a liability for him. You should keep careful track of your active cases, and report the discharges to your surety company as they come from the court.

Discharges are important to inform your surety company of cases being finally adjudicated. When the times comes for you to ask for your money back from your Build-Up Fund, you will only get it if your bonds have been discharged on a regular basis.

Management of Client Data

If you make your business grow and become successful, you will have extensive files on your customers. You will need to access the data and report it to your surety insurance company and the regulator.

There are a number of software packages that have been developed for the bail bond business. One such system is actually Internet based, with access through your modem.

You should make the investment early in a good software package so that you can track your customers and generate reports for your surety insurance company and the state regulator with just a few keystrokes.

Records retention requirements will vary by state, but a typical state insurance department requirement is that you keep records on all transactions for five years. The IRS requires retention for three years, but the five-year rule is probably a better standard.

Advertising and Promotion

Yellow Pages Advertising

Yellow Pages Advertising can make or break your business. People who refer to the *Yellow Pages* are important to you because:

1. Customers need you
2. They are ready to buy
3. You have what they want
4. You are ready when they want it

Yes, these are the people whom you want to service, but can you afford the cost of the *Yellow Pages* advertising?

Bail bond companies are fifth or sixth on the list of businesses that spend the most money on this kind of promotion, after lawyers, doctors, heating and air conditioning, etc. This is a somewhat proven method of advertising, but it is not the only one.

Can you afford the cost of advertising? In many markets, the standard for bail bond advertising is at least a full-page advertisement, if not a double-truck (two page) ad. With costs of $10,000 *per month per page*, this type of advertising is probably not in the budget of a start-up bail bond agency. The bills for *Yellow Pages* advertising can easily break your business!

If you do go the route of significant investment in the *Yellow Pages*, be sure to use the services of a *Yellow Pages* advertising agency. They will design your ads and negotiate lower monthly rates. You could look at Guaranteed Marketing, Inc. www.yellowpagesprofit.com as an example, or you could Google "Yellow Page Advertising" and receive a nearly unending list of these advertising agencies.

The greatest word of caution that I can give to you is not to overspend on *Yellow Pages*. There are many other ways to advertise, and a number of proven techniques are given here. There are alternatives to turning all of your green dollar bills into yellow pages in the telephone book.

Used U-Haul Trucks

One of the most innovative advertising ideas that I have seen recently is the use of used rental trucks as mobile advertising. Patriot Truck Leasing www.patriottruckleasing.com, a separately owned division of U-Haul's parent, will provide trucks and graphics on a monthly lease basis. The trucks are deemed not road-worthy for long interstate travel, but are still registered, insured, and can travel locally.

Prices range from $500 to $1,000 for the graphics, and leasing fees start at $244.95 per month. The deal works month-to-month, with no long-term commitment. Patriot is responsible for all vehicle maintenance.

How should the truck be used? It is a giant mobile billboard, that can be parked anywhere (beware of restrictions on advertising close to jails or courts). Be sure to move it regularly to maintain it as a vehicle, as opposed to a stationary billboard. If your town or city has parades (Fourth of July, Labor Day, etc.) volunteer your truck to pull floats. If you think about various uses, the list will become very long.

Jail Postings and Sign Boards

In some jurisdictions, the jail will post a list of local bail bond agencies. Alternatively, the jail may have small advertising boards (meaning you pay the jail a fee to have your name and telephone number posted) to list the names.

It is important that the name of your business is posted at the jail, if allowed. When an inmate is calling family or friends, your name and telephone number can be right in front of his eyes!

Collect Calls and Toll-Free Numbers

I have never understood why bail agencies refused collect calls from defendants in jail! Here you have a customer looking for service, and his call is refused. You might as well put up a sign that says, "Don't bother to call us!"

In the typical jail, a defendant can only make collect calls on the institution's phones. Perhaps in the booking room there might be a pay telephone that allows toll-free number calls.

When I started my bail bond business, none of my competitors accepted collect calls or had toll-free numbers. I advertised the toll-free number, along with the statement "Collect Calls Accepted". My telephone began ringing on the very first day, and has not stopped ringing.

If a defendant calls collect or on your toll-free number from the jail, you want to talk to him. Accept the charges (usually less than $5 total), and the odds are very high that you could earn $1,000 in bail bond fees. That sounds like a great investment to me!

Billboards

Good old ugly billboards! I love billboards, but some states hate them so much that billboards have been outlawed. I remember the old saying, "Anything that's good must be unethical, immoral or illegal". Billboards are good, especially near the jails or the courthouses (again, watch for restrictions about advertising near the jails).

Not as expensive as *Yellow Pages* advertising, billboards can produce great results. Whether the billboards are huge, fifty-foot advertisements on top of a building, or small 3' by 4' signs in kiosks at bus stops, you are best off using an agency to help design and place the advertising. You could look at Global Outdoor Services (www.billboards.com), check the web site of the Outdoor Advertising Association of America, Inc. (www.oaaa.org), or Google "billboards" for another unending list.

Internet

Yes, the Internet is the present and the future. However, I had an individual web site for my company for a number of years and never got a single referral from it. I did, however, receive referrals from other services that specialize solely in forwarding business to bail bond companies.

For instance, you could look at www.bailbond.com as an example of this type of service. Started by Russell Faibisch, one of the leading national managing general agents, this internet site provides many different types of services for bail agencies, including referrals, bond postings, real estate evaluation, publication of fugitive information, etc.

Bumper Stickers

I started my bumper sticker campaign as a joke! During a PBUS (www.pbus.com) convention, a fellow bail agent showed me his version of the bumper sticker.

I created a sticker that parodies the concept of: "My Child is Student of the Month at Jones Elementary School". My bumper sticker says:

"My Child is Inmate of the Month at the County Jail", then lists the bail agency name and toll-free telephone number.

The bumper stickers were in demand not by customers, but by police, jail and court personnel! I really did not care who put them on the cars, as long as my business got the exposure.

Give-Aways

I always had something in my briefcase to give away to customers, law enforcement, jail personnel, etc.

My favorite Give-Away was pens. I would have Bic plastic pens printed with the business name and toll-free telephone number and freely hand out bunches of them wherever I went. Each year, I would give away almost 5,000 pens, which people carried in their purses or pockets. At approximately thirty cents per pen, it was wonderfully cheap advertising.

I knew that my pen campaign was successful when I went to the local bank to make a deposit, and I was handed one of my own pens to endorse the check!

Also popular with law enforcement and jail personnel were pocket calendars and mini-handcuff key chains.

Each December, I would freely distribute the pocket calendars, embossed with my business name and toll-free telephone number. As the end of the year approached, I would be repeatedly asked for this item.

The mini-handcuffs were in demand all year! "I'm going to a bachelorette party! Can I have some hand-cuffs?" Needless to say, each set of cuffs had a tag with the business name and toll-free telephone number.

It may sound as though I was giving away trashy items. Well, these items became very popular and created significant good will among people who could spread my business's name by word of mouth. I cannot count the number of times I received a bail telephone call from someone who was reading the number off of a pen, pocket calendar, or mini-handcuff!

Community Networking

Speaking at the Rotary Club, PTA, etc. sounds like an unlikely strategy for a bail agent. However, everyone really does want to know about the bail business, even if they are not regular customers. Also, you must remember that the most respected members of your community may one day run afoul of the DWI laws, or have a family member or employee who ends up in jail. I had one company owner who almost monthly was bailing out one or another of his employees.

The secret to being invited to speak is subtlety. Send all of the organizations a letter saying that you are willing on short notice to speak about bail if the scheduled speaker should cancel for any reason. Usually these types of organizations have someone who recruits speakers, and you have just given him a gift! Your telephone will ring with many invitations to speak.

When you are in front of the audience, talk about bail, but also talk about other services that you can provide to the community. I know a woman bail agent who regularly talks to the PTA about her drug and alcohol testing services. Her philosophy is that if parents come to her office now for testing of a child, they will come to her office for a bail bond when the child is arrested for drug-related crimes.

If this drug testing aspect interests you, visit the Omega Laboratories (www.omegalabs.net) web site. PBUS (www.pbus.com) has signed a contract for reduced rates to bail agents. For a more extensive review of drug testing, see the chapter on **Related Businesses**.

Rewards for Fugitives and Wanted Posters

In the very next chapter, I will talk about **When It All Goes Wrong** and what happens when you have FTA's, forfeitures and fugitives. It seems hard to believe that rewards for fugitives and wanted posters can help promote your bail agency, but it is an extremely effective technique.

One defendant for whom I posted bail ran off with his underage girlfriend. Local police, along with the FBI, began looking for the defendant. As it turned out, the booking camera at the local police station had malfunctioned, and my bail agency was the only source for an appropriate picture of the defendant. Of course, we cooperated with the police.

After a week, with no sign of the defendant or the underage girlfriend, I offered a $5,000 reward for information leading to the capture of the defendant. I faxed copies of a news release and a wanted poster to the statewide newspapers and the TV stations. What do you think happened?

Of course, each and every newspaper carried an article about the reward, along with an interview with me. Additionally, the TV station interviewed me in front of the jail, and broadcast my name and my bail agency's name across the state.

What great publicity and exposure I received for offering that reward! Now you are wondering, did I have to pay the $5,000? The police captured the defendant and his underage girlfriend, so I made a donation of $500 to the local police athletic league. But the publicity was worth tens of thousands of dollars.

Going to the Courthouse With A Big Check

Yes, you will eventually pay forfeited bails. But you can derive positive publicity from this financial loss!

When paying a forfeited bail, most bail agents either mail a check or quietly slip in the back door of the courthouse. They do not want the world to know that they "failed" and must pay a bail.

I take the opposite view. In the section on **Obligations of the Bail Agent**, I state that one of those obligations is to pay the bail when a defendant cannot be returned to custody. Paying the bail is not a failure; it is just another way to successfully complete the job!

Reserve the following strategy for a larger forfeiture, something like $10,000 or $25,000. When you have exhausted every attempt to recapture a fugitive, prepare to write the check. But, first, you need to publicize the fact that you will be going to the courthouse to make a big payment on a forfeited bail. Send out news releases saying when you will be at the courthouse with the check. Invite the press to take pictures.

The day you go to the courthouse, expect to see reporters and photographers. Hold up the check so they can take pictures showing your payment of $10,00, $25,000 or more. Ask the Clerk of Court to pose for the photographers, receiving your check. Finally, be sure to offer the press many of the details on your unsuccessful attempt to return the defendant.

I had a defendant who absconded to the US Virgin Islands. My bail enforcement agent located him and arranged for his arrest by the US Marshal Service. The local Sheriff sent two deputies to the Virgin Islands to bring back the defendant. I paid the bills, but all of this was chronicled by the statewide newspaper and TV station. Again, this was great publicity for my business.

Use a loss to make a gain!

When It All Goes Wrong

"If You Write Bail, You Will Have Forfeitures"

During my early years in bail, I agonized over each and every FTA that I received. I reviewed each file, and asked myself the question, "What did I do wrong?"

I reviewed and discussed my underwriting guidelines with my bail enforcement agent. Why was I getting FTA's? His answer was very simple: "If you write bail, you will have forfeitures".

It took me a while to embrace that philosophy, but I came to realize the truth of the statement. No matter how good a bail might look when you sign the bail bond, never be surprised when the FTA notice arrives in the mail.

You must understand that forfeitures are a common element in the bail bond business, and you must be prepared to deal with them. Accept a forfeiture as a part of doing business, in the same way that an automobile rental company sees dented fenders as a part of doing business.

In the section on **The Bail Agent's Right of Arrest**, we discussed the historical derivation of the authority to re-arrest a fugitive. Now we will discuss the practical aspects.

Bail Enforcement Agent (Bounty Hunter)

Is bail enforcement and apprehension of fugitives going to be done by you, your employee, or a contractor? Almost weekly, I received telephone calls from people who wanted to become Bounty Hunters. There are more "Wannabees" in this business than I can count. You need to tread carefully in this area.

Experience counts for more than anything else in bail enforcement. This is the one area where a wrong step can get you sued for millions of dollars, put you out of the business and eventually bankrupt you. If you do not personally have experience in bail enforcement and apprehension, look for someone who does.

Beware of the Weekend Wonders! Many people are making a good living by running weekend schools on "How to Become A Bounty Hunter". These are like factories, turning out over-eager and inexperienced "Wannabees" who will only get you and your business into trouble.

Seek out the local, experienced bail enforcement agent and use his services. Learn about his history and measure his experience.

I have heard many stories of "Wannabees" who have gone to the local courthouse trying to get a list of FTA's. They want to go out searching for your fugitive and apprehend him without your approval, expecting that you will pay them a fee for the recovery.

To protect yourself, you should take the following steps:

1. Make it clear to everyone, especially local law enforcement, that you use one specific bail enforcement agent or company.

2. Provide that bail enforcement agent with *written* authority to make the apprehension on your behalf.

3. Ask the bail enforcement agent to leave a copy of that written authority with the police for their files.

One of the simplest and best written authorizations that I have seen is the Bail Recovery Agent Contract commonly used in the State of Washington www.dol.wa.gov/forms/692011.pdf. Use this contract, or something similar, to protect yourself from the threat of liability that could be incurred by inexperienced "Wannabees".

In real estate investing, the three key words are, "Location, Location, and Location". In bail recovery, the three key words are, "Liability, Liability, and Liability".

Licensing and insurance are also very specific concerns. Make sure that your bail recovery agent is properly licensed and insured, if required by your state.

Extradition Limitations

Although many bail agents and bail recovery agents ignore them, there are very serious limitations on the ability to transport a fugitive across state lines to return him to the jurisdiction from which he fled.

When an FTA occurs, the court will issue a warrant for the defendant's arrest. The local sheriff may (or may not) enter the warrant into the National Crime Information Center (NCIC) computer system. This is the system that gets checked every time you are stopped for speeding, are arrested, or have almost any other interaction with the police. Always check with the local sheriff to make sure that the warrant has been entered into NCIC.

It is very important to know that only felony warrants are accepted in the NCIC system. If your fugitive is wanted on a misdemeanor, it will not be entered into NCIC (I have tried many times), which makes interstate apprehension very difficult.

The *Uniform Criminal Extradition Act* (UCEA) was passed as model legislation by Congress, and has been adopted by almost every state. Many states have begun interpreting the UCEA to mean that a bail recovery agent must surrender the defendant to local law enforcement for traditional extradition process, and cannot be transported across state lines without his permission.

What happened to <u>Taylor v. Taintor</u>? A discussed in the chapter on **A Short History of Bail**, states have legislated or handed down court decisions limiting the interstate transportation of fugitives.

A good example is the Commonwealth of Massachusetts. In the case of <u>Commonwealth v. Lance Wilkinson, et al; 613 N.E.914 Mass. 1993</u>, the Supreme Judicial Court of the Commonwealth ruled that the UCEA applied to bail recovery agents, as well as typical law enforcement authorities. The Court ruled that a defendant could not be denied the right to extradition.

One of the leading attorneys in this area of law is Milton Hirsch of Miami, Florida. Attorney Hirsch has given presentations to the Professional Bail Agents of the United States and many state bail associations at their conventions. See the list of **Miscellaneous Contacts** for contact information for Attorney Hirsch.

Making Your Business Grow

Agents and Sub-Agents

There is really only one key resource to make your business grow: People! You must bring people into the bail bond business, working for you. You will train them, support them, pay them, and perhaps fire them, but you must bring people into the business.

Many bail agents believe that employees represent two things: problems and future competition. To a certain extent, this is correct, but the problems are usually more than offset by the extra income that you will make. As regards training competition, you will be surprised at the huge percentage of people who do not want the long-term on-going responsibility of running a business. Remember, there will be those weeks when, after having paid your employees, there is no money left for you!

The truly successful people in this business, the ones who are making the most money, are bail agents who have many sub-agents, or who have grown enough to become managing general agents. As an MGA, you make a small amount of money from each agent, but, if you have many agents, you make a lot of money overall.

You should look to do business in every area of your state. Bring on sub-agents who will do the actual work at the jail while you control the underwriting from a central office. Have your toll-free number in every telephone book, but have it ring in your personal office. You can then dispatch sub-agents to the appropriate jail to meet with indemnitors and post bonds.

Eventually, your business will become so large and so busy that you cannot handle the volume of calls. Besides, we all need a vacation or a day off!

This is the point at which you begin to make yourself into a managing general agent. Take the best employee in the most distant office, and offer them the opportunity make that business their own. Make them liable for every bond that they write, have a build-up fund for them, and charge them a little extra for bond cost. Perhaps your surety insurance company will even cut the rate it charges because of your heightened volume.

Suddenly, you have become a managing general agent. If you do this enough times, you can make an astounding amount of money!

The Owner Should NOT Run The Business

Yes, that's right, I believe that the owner, the general agent, should not run the business. That is why you have trained employees, to do all of the day-to-day work.

After a bail bond business has been properly established, probably after two or three years, the general agent's first priority is to make the business grow. This means that instead of doing a weekly payroll, an employee acts as payroll clerk. Your much more valuable time is spent interacting with potentially new agents, meeting with lobbyists, buying agencies, etc.

When I brought my first sub-agent into the business, I resented giving her a substantial paycheck for work that I could easily have done myself. But I soon came to realize the benefits of the days off, vacations, lobbying, negotiating, and just plain uninterrupted time to think.

Yes, when you hire employees you are hiring problems and training the competition. But employees are the key element to making your business grow and making you an ever-increasing income.

Other Bonding Opportunities

Immigration Bonds

How many sections of this book have begun with the words, "DON'T DO IT!" Well, immigration bonds represent a small niche in the bail bond business that you should probably avoid. Most surety insurance companies will not let you do this type of bond.

Typically, an immigration bond is posted for an alien who is subject to deportation proceedings. The bonds are posted to guarantee the appearance of the alien at his deportation trial before an immigration judge.

Some estimates are as high as 80% of the bonds are breached (the immigration jargon for an FTA). Whatever estimate you use, the breach rate is huge compared to criminal bail bonds. Let's face it, if you are going to be deported to some extremely poor nation in Africa, Asia, or South America, you are willing to do or pay almost anything to avoid that fate.

The immigration bond business is highly specialized, and seems to be restricted geographically to California, Texas, New York and Florida. The typical immigration bond agency does only immigration bonds, is multi-lingual, and collateralizes the bonds by as much as 200%.

In the 1990's, I thought of immigration bonds as a way to expand my business in New England. I did a total of one bond, spending a week's worth of my valuable time to earn very little. I quickly gave up the immigration bond business.

Court Bonds

Court bonds are a guarantee to that court that something will be done. For example, in a civil suit where $10 million dollars has been awarded to the plaintiff, the defendant may appeal the case, but the court requires a guarantee, a bond, that the $10 million will be available to the plaintiff before allowing the appeal.

In the Appendix, you will find a copy of a court bond that was done by American Contractors Indemnity Company, a division of HCC Surety Group www.hccsurety.com (see contact information in the **Short List of Surety Companies and Contacts**), for $30 million, with a premium of $938,000. The agent retained somewhere around 20% of the premium, and had no liability if the bond were forfeited.

You can find opportunities for court bonds through the probate courts and other civil courts. Discuss the process with an experienced surety company before attempting to solicit this business.

Child Custody Bonds

Child Custody Bonds were developed by PBUS, in association with the National Center for Missing and Exploited Children www.missingkids.com. The intent of the bonds is to provide a guarantee that a separated parent or other family member taking custody of children for an international trip or other circumstance will return the children to the parent with legal custody.

Child kidnapping by a non-custodial parent is a very significant issue. Many times, a non-custodial parent taking a child on an international trip does not buy a return ticket. He has taken the children and the custodial parent has little or no recourse.

Although the bond exists and surety companies can be found to write it, there has been little to no demand since it's development in 2000. However, you should keep an eye on this market and be prepared to provide bonds if it should develop.

Visa Bonds and Guest Worker Bonds

The events of 9/11 and the resultant "War on Terror" have generated a plethora of federal legislation. In the area of immigration, Congress has been discussing visa bonds and guest worker bonds.

A visa bond would provide a financial guarantee that an immigrant in the United States on a work visa (typically a three year visa) would properly leave the country at the end of his approved stay. Work visas are usually restricted to highly educated, valuable employees, such as doctors, engineers, etc.

A guest worker bond could be implemented under the legislation proposed to deal with the ten (or is it twelve? Maybe it's fifteen!) million illegal aliens in this country. Regardless of the true number of illegal aliens, this is a potentially huge market for the bail bond business.

Neither visa bonds nor guest worker bonds are part of law as of this writing. However, you should keep a very close eye on this legislation, because it represents a potentially huge market for the bail bond business.

Related Businesses

GPS Tracking

Over the past few years, the development of GPS tracking has been applied to sex offenders, parolees and probationers. The success of this new style of monitoring and supervision has convinced many judges and local jails to begin using it for pre-trial releases.

It is my belief that GPS tracking is a technological tsunami that will engulf all types of incarceration (pre-trial and post-conviction). As the months and years go by, we will see more and more use of this technology.

The serious thinkers in the bail bond business have been pushing bail agents to embrace this market, combining a GPS tracking unit with a bail bond. This hybrid type of business is certainly the future.

PBUS is currently negotiating nation-wide contracts with GPS companies on behalf of bail agents. To learn more about the technology, you can visit the web site of iSecuretrac Corporation at www.isecuretrac.com.

Electronic Monitoring

Many people confuse GPS tracking with electronic monitoring. I differentiate the two technologies this way:

1. GPS tracking does what its name implies; the technology uses global positioning satellites to locate and track the whereabouts of a subject.

2. Electronic monitoring, however, may not tell you where the subject is, but it will tell you if he is using alcohol, drugs, etc.

A great example of electronic monitoring is a device distributed by Alcohol Monitoring Systems, Inc. www.alcoholmonitoring.com. It is extremely common for a parole, probation or pre-trial release subject to be prohibited from using alcohol. This ankle bracelet tests a defendant's perspiration every few minutes, looking for traces of alcohol. The device reports violation, dates and times to the court for appropriate action.

It is important to understand that the courts and corrections departments are using GPS tracking and electronic monitoring not to just locate a defendant, but to change his behavior. You must keep your attention on this growing trend of behavioral change, and factor it into your business decisions.

Drug/Alcohol/DNA Testing

CSI Las Vegas, Forensic Files and other criminal science TV shows have made the general population very aware of science as applied to criminal behavior. As mentioned in the chapter **Advertising and Promotion**, one bail agent speaks to PTA groups and other children-oriented organizations about drug and alcohol testing that she does in her office. Her feeling is that if the parents bring in a child for drug testing, they will also come to her for a bail bond.

Drug and alcohol testing used to be completely urine based, which could be a pretty nasty business. Other avenues have been developed, particularly using a snippet of hair as the basis for the test.

PBUS has signed a contract with Omega Laboratories, Inc. www.omegalabs.net to provide reduced rates for testing. Your job is to provide the snippet of hair and a signed liability release, and Omega does the testing.

The concept here is to generate traffic into your office among people who probably will need a bail bond in the future. Although you do not make a huge sum on each test, these potential clients have come to know you.

Western Union

When I opened my check cashing operation (which I will explain in the next section), I became a Western Union www.westernunion.com agent. What a convenience! Suddenly, I was able to have people wire money to me, I could have my check cashing store cut a check, and I could go straight to the jail and bail the defendant, picking up the check later.

If you have opened an office near the local jail, you should become a Western Union Agent and hang one of their neon signs in your window. Many people are receiving money to pay a bail bondsman via a Western Union money transfer, and you will get their attention with the neon sign.

This additional business will make a little money for you, but it will increase the traffic in your office dramatically. To become a Western Union, send email to the company at moneytransfer@westernunion.com.

Check Cashing and Payday Loans

Check cashing and Payday loans are another way to make lots of money and increase your bail business at the same time.

I started my check cashing business in 1998, as a totally separate business. However, many people knew me as the bail bondsman, so they told their friends, and vice versa. My suggestion is that you start this business next door to your bail office, in the abutting storefront and make it clear that the two businesses are related. Perhaps a common entrance would work best.

The national association of check cashers is called the Financial Service Corporations of America www.fisca.org, which has a really tremendous annual conference where you can learn about the business and talk to literally hundreds of vendors.

Here are a couple of vendors:
1. www.idealss.com
2. www.paydayplus.com
3. www.citylightbulletproof.com
4. www.biopay.com
5. www.cellcards.net

Electronic Filing/Tax Preparation

I really wanted to do tax return preparation and electronic filing, but I never had the time to get it going. I know one bail agent in Jacksonville, Florida who does almost 1,000 returns each year, netting about $30 per return. However, the real money is made in the tax refund anticipation loans, where the taxpayer pays a significant fee to get his tax refund essentially immediately. One of the leaders in this business is Drake Software www.drakesoftware.com.

A General Comment About Related Businesses

I believe that all of these related businesses will help to enhance your bail bond business. But it is important to keep your eye on the ball: you are in business to make money, and your time is very valuable. If one of these businesses is not producing customers and profits, dump it. Cut your losses early rather than throwing money into a black hole.

Associations, Education and Networking

Professional Bail Agents of the United States

The Professional Bail Agents of the United States (PBUS), the national association representing the estimated 14,000 bail agents, has an office located in Washington, DC, housing an Executive Director and support staff. Overseen by a Board of Directors elected from association members, the mission of the association is stated on its web site (www.pbus.com):

The mission of the Professional Bail Agents of the United States (PBUS) is to provide Information, Education and Representation for the 14,000 bail agents nationwide.

If you have any serious intention of starting a bail bond business, you should become involved with PBUS from the very beginning. The association holds conventions in February and July. The February meeting is always in Las Vegas, and the July meeting is usually held in a resort-type destination.

Why should you belong to PBUS?

The association can be a real fountain of information when you are establishing and expanding your business. At the meetings, you can learn about surety insurance companies, meet Managing General Agents, see the latest software, meet vendors of all sorts, etc.

From an education point of view, PBUS offers programs leading to the professional designation of Certified Bail Agent (CBA) and Certified Recovery Agent (CRA). Got a bail-related problem? Some member of PBUS has probably had the same problem, and can provide you with a solution.

As an advocate for the bail business, PBUS has worked on federal legislation, and worked with state associations for state legislation. With its publications and political connections, there is no stronger voice for the general bail bond community.

I have been a member of PBUS since my very first year in the business. I strongly urge you to attend a convention *before you start your business* so that you can make the right connections at the very beginning.

In the list of **Miscellaneous Contacts**, I have provided all of the contact information for PBUS.

State-wide And Local Associations

As you have learned from earlier sections of this book, the bail bond business is regulated at the state and local level. It is important to always be aware of new legislative proposals in your state that may affect your business.

State and local associations monitor legislation, provide continuing education, and are a voice for your state's bail bond community.

In some of the larger markets, very strong and effective state associations have developed. For example, look at the web sites of the California Bail Agents Association (www.cbaa.com), the Professional Bondsmen of Texas (www.pbtx.com), the Florida Surety Agents Association (www.fsaa.com), Arkansas Professional Bail Association (http://www.arkansasbail.com), Mississippi (http://www.msbail.org), North Carolina (http://www.ncbaa.com), or Washington State (http://www.wsbaa.com).

It is at these state and local association meetings that you will learn the particular nuances of your state's bail market. Attend at least one meeting before starting your new business.

Surety Company Conventions

Some, but not all, surety insurance companies will have conventions for their agents each year. Again, these conventions can be the place to learn many things about the business.

If you are considering signing a contract with a surety insurance company, ask if there is an upcoming annual convention. If so, can you attend the convention *before* you sign a contract? This will give you the opportunity to talk discreetly with other agents of the company about how good (or bad) the support of the company really is.

As a newcomer to the industry, you will be amazed at how open and welcoming most of these national, state and local associations are. They will provide you with the opportunity to learn and network about the bail bond business. If at all possible, attend these meetings *before* starting your business, so that you have the proper insights into the profession that you will be entering.

Valuing and Selling Your Bail Agency

To Whom Can You Sell?

It may seem ironic that a book on "How To Start A Bail Bond Business" should include a chapter on **Valuing and Selling Your Bail Agency**. However, before entering a business, you should always determine how you would be able to exit the business.

My father always told me, when in public, sit with my back to the wall so that I could see trouble coming. Well, exiting the bail bond business could be one of those troubling things that you need to see coming at you, and not sneaking up behind you.

The issue revolves around all of those bonds that you were writing in the years leading up to the sale of your business. Since your business only has value if it is on-going, you need to continue writing bail right up to your last day as owner. But who will take care of discharging the bonds, recovering fugitives, and paying forfeitures? After all, your surety insurance company contract says that you are personally liable for all forfeitures on bonds that you wrote. To get your Build-Up Fund back, you will have to prove that all of your bonds have been discharged, which means that you will not receive the money until two, three, or even four years after the sale.

You can sell your bail agency to anyone, but the sale may end up costing you more money than the sales price, and the total loss of your Build-Up Fund, if your bond obligations are not properly managed.

To Whom SHOULD You Sell?

The most challenging question that you will face when selling your business is not just the selling price, but the considerations of your bond liability. This means that you cannot just sell the business to any potential buyer; you must sell the business to someone whom you can trust to properly discharge your bond liability.

There are only two types of people to whom you can sell your business: a relative or a trusted experienced employee.

Keeping the business in the family is usually the best route to go. If a child or other close relative has been working in the business, or wants to work in the business, you should embrace him as a potential buyer. Particularly with a child, you know that he will work for your benefit.

If there is no family member interested in the business, you have to turn to your most loyal and trusted employee. If you give them a reasonable deal on the selling price, will they work for your benefit?

These are the kinds of considerations that you have when you are trying to find a buyer. You must think about this very carefully, and develop your family member or trusted employee in the business well before approaching them about the sale.

What's It Worth?

I can sense your mind working, trying to determine a price for a medium-sized, profitable bail agency. The prices that I have seen have been all over the map, depending upon circumstances.

I have seen agencies sold for as much as $36 million (yes, that's $36,000,000) and for as little as nothing. I personally bought a medium-sized but profitable agency in another state that was in a very distressed situation for $1,000.

I believe a fair price for an agency is the equivalent of one year's gross revenues, usually paid over time. The typical buyer does not have a huge lump of money to pay to you up-front.

Let's use an example: ABC Bail Agency is writing $10 million in penal amount each year, which means that the gross revenues are $1 million. A reasonable purchase price is $1 million, paid in equal installments from the monthly gross revenue over a five-year period of time. Alternatively, 20% of the gross revenues paid monthly will make the buyer feel more comfortable, as the final price will vary as business rises and falls.

If You REALLY, REALLY Need To Sell Now

Life is full of surprises, and few of them are pleasant. Illness, bankruptcy, or even death may require the immediate sale of your business. Whom should you call?

If you have attended PBUS and local state association conventions, you have met some managing general agents and surety insurance company representatives. These are the contacts that will help you to locate an immediate and experienced buyer. Perhaps they might even buy the business themselves.

To sum up this chapter, you must always have a succession plan in mind, from the day you start the business until the day you finally walk out the door. Begin thinking about it now!

Miscellaneous Contacts

Professional Bail Agents of the United States (PBUS)

Web Site: www.pbus.com

Stephen Kreimer, Executive Director

skreimer@pbus.com

1301 Pennsylvania Avenue NW, Suite 925

Washington, DC 20004

(800) 883-PBUS

Fidelity Insurance Bond (if you cannot find one in your state)

National Insurance Group

PO Box 379

New Albany, Indiana 47151

(812) 945-2321

Credit Card Processing, American Spirit Processing, Inc.

Web Site: www.americanspiritprocessing.com

James M. Peeler, President

sales@americanspiritprocessing.com

PO Box 916028

Longwood, Florida 32791-6028

(800) 877-2964

Milton Hirsch, PA

Attorney Milton Hirsch

Two Datran Center, Suite 1504

9130 South Dadeland Boulevard

Miami, Florida 33156

Money Transfers and Money Orders

Web Site: www.westernunion.com

Western Union

moneytransfer@westernunion.com

12500 E. Belford Avenue, #M2288

Englewood, California 80112-5939

(800) 354-0005 Press 0

Electronic Check Services

Web Site: www.advantagepaymentsys.com

Advantage ACH-EFT & Electronic Check Services

2920 Regatta Drive, Suite 102

Las Vegas, Nevada 89128-6892

(888) 718-6767

Check Cashers' Association

Web Site: www.fisca.org

Financial Service Centers of America, Inc.

PO Box 647

Hackensack, New Jersey 07602-0647

(201) 487-0412

High Risk Consumer Information

Web Site: www.teletrack.com

Tele-Track, Inc.

155 Technology Parkway, Suite 800

Norcross, Georgia 30092-2962

(800) 729-6981

Check Cashing and Pay Day Loan Software

Web Site: www.idealss.com

Ideal Software Systems, Inc.

PO Box 3065

Meridian, Mississippi 39303-3065

(800) 964-3325

Pre-Paid Phone Cards

Web Site: www.cellcards.net

CellCards of Illinois

2720 River Road, Suite 18

Des Plaines, Illinois 60018-4109

(877) 230-8300 extension 3207

California Bail Agents Association

Web Site: www.cbaa.com

Florida Surety Agents Association

Web Site: www.fsaa.com

Professional Bondsmen of Texas

Web Site: www.pbtx.com

Arkansas Professional Bail Association

Web Site: www.arkansasbail.com

Mississippi Bail Association

Web Site: www.msbail.org

North Carolina Bail Association

Web Site: www.ncbaa.com

Washington State Bail Association

Web Site: www.wsbaa.com

A Short List of Surety Companies

I have put Roche Surety and Casualty Company at the top of my list of suggested surety insurance companies because **Judi Aultman** represents Roche. Judi is the regional manager (mentioned in the introduction) who put me into the bail bond business so many years ago.

Roche Surety and Casualty Company

Web Site: www.rochesurety.com

1910 Orient Road

Tampa, Florida 33619

Judi Aultman: judi@rochesurety.com; (317) 481-1307

Shannon Roche: Shannon@rochesurety.com; (813) 623-5042

As President of the Connecticut State Surety Association and Treasurer of the Professional Bail Agents of the United States, **Mary Casey** has come to be recognized as one of the most knowledgeable and effective leaders in the Bail Bond Business today.

American Surety Company

Web Site: www.americansuretycompany.com

PO Box 68932

Indianapolis, Indiana 46268

Mary Casey: mcasey02@earthlink.net; (860) 459-9453

As a National Managing General Agent, **Russell Faibisch** and his agency Surety Corporation of America have more than four decades of experience in bail. His organization is very innovative and very supportive of new agents.

Surety Corporation of America

Russell Faibisch, National Managing General Agent

1000 NW 14th Street

Miami, Florida 33136

Web Site: www.bailbond.com

Russell Faibisch russell@bailbonds.com (305) 512-7676

Mark Heffernan mark@bailbonds.com; (305) 525-1434

Bill Kreins and Safety National Insurance Corporation have been long-time supporters of PBUS and the many state associations. Bill has taken leadership responsibilities in dealing with important issues affecting bail agents, from federal legislation to GPS Tracking.

Safety National Corporation

P.O. Box 445

Alto, New Mexico 88312

Bill Kreins **sudie10@valornet.com**; (505) 336-1096

Linda Braswell is a managing general agent for Lexington National Insurance Corporation. She is a Past President of the Florida Surety Agents Association and President of the Professional Bail Agents of the United

States (PBUS). Linda is probably the most highly respected woman in bail today.

Lexington National Insurance Corp.

Web Site: www.lexingtonnational.com

200 East Lexington Street, Ste. 501

Baltimore, Maryland 21202

Linda Braswell: braswellss@aol.com; (772) 287-2869

HCC Surety Group and **Fred Anschultz** are very supportive of the national and state bail organizations, and hve urged agents to diversify into other related areas such as court bonds. Led by an innovative group of insurance professionals, the company is a leader in the bail bond business.

HCC Surety Group

9841 Airport Boulevard, 9th Floor

Los Angeles California 90045

Fred Anschultz fanschultz@hccsurety.com; (310) 649-2663

International Fidelity Insurance Company is the largest surety company in the bail bond business, and has been supporting bail for decades. **Ed Sheppard**, regional manager for the company, has been involved in every aspect of the business, from starting agencies to apprehending fugitives.

International Fidelity Insurance Company

Web Site: www.aiasurety.com

9000 SW 94th Street

Miami, Florida 33176

Phone: (800) 938-2245   (305) 596-9878

Edward Sheppard ed.sheppard@aiasurety.com

Forms

1. <u>Application For Appearance Bond</u> – Distributed by AMWEST Surety Insurance Company, this is one of the best data collecting forms that I have seen in the Bail Bond Business. The four page form is printed on an 11" by 17" piece of paper, and folded to make a folder for all of the customer information. The first two pages include the defendant information, and the last two pages are indemnitor information.

2. <u>Assignment Of Savings Account</u> – On occasion, you will be offered a bank savings account or certificate of deposit as collateral for a bail. This assignment form, again distributed by AMWEST, is used to inform the bank, and to get an acknowledgement that includes the bank stamp. The form is completed in duplicate, one for the bank and one for you.

3. <u>Mortgage Form</u> – This form is provided only as an example! Proper mortgage documents vary by state, so be sure to have your attorney prepare an appropriate mortgage for you.

4. <u>Collateral and Fee Receipt</u> – Most surety insurance companies provide you with a combined fee receipt, collateral receipt, and bail bond in one numbered form for accountability purposes. Some companies provide little books of bail bonds, and you need to contrive your own receipt. This is an example of a collateral and fee receipt used with the book-style bail bonds.

5. <u>New Hampshire Court Bail Bond</u> – Not to be confused with the bail bond form that you give to the court, this form is a standardized court

bond used in every case, and is signed by the defendant, bail agent (Surety), and the Bail Commissioner or Clerk of Court.

6. <u>Vermont Court Appearance (Bail) Bond</u> – Again, not to be confused with the bail bond form that you give to the court, this is a standardized court bond used in every case, and is signed by the defendant and the bail agent (surety).

7. <u>Vermont Conditions Of Release Order</u> – In addition to a court bail bond, most courts set conditions of release that, if violated, can send the defendant back to jail. This Vermont Conditions of Release Order is a typical example.

APPLICATION FOR APPEARANCE BOND
BAIL BONDS, Inc.

DEFENDANT _____

AGENT _____

POWER NO. _____

CAUSE NO. _____

I, the undersigned, do hereby apply to you to act as my bail in the amount of $ _____

in the _____ Court of _____ wherein I am

EXECUTION DATE _____

CONTACT BY _____

charged with _____

ADDRESS _____

and I agree to the following terms and conditions prescribed by the State Insurance Department.

DATE _____ TIME _____

TERMS AND CONDITIONS

RELATIONSHIP _____

The following terms and conditions are an integral part of this application for appearance bond No. _____ dated _____ for which BAIL BONDS, Inc., or its Agent shall receive a premium in the amount of _____ Dollars ($ _____) and the parties agree that said appearance bond is conditioned upon full compliance of all said terms and conditions and is a part of said bond and application therefor.

1. BAIL BONDS, Inc., as bail, shall have control and jurisdiction over the Defendant during the term for which the bond is executed and shall have the right to apprehend, arrest and surrender the Defendant to the proper officials at any time as provided by law.

2. In the event surrender of Defendant is made prior to the time set for Defendant's appearances, and for reason other than as enumerated below in paragraph 3, then Defendant shall be entitled to a refund of the bond premium.

3. It is understood and agreed that the happening of any one of the following events shall constitute a breach of Defendant's obligations to BAIL BONDS, Inc. hereunder, and BAIL BONDS, Inc. shall have the right to forthwith apprehend, arrest, and surrender Defendant, and defendant shall have no right to any refund of premium whatsoever. Said events which shall constitute a breach of Defendant's obligations hereunder are:
    (a) If Defendant shall depart the jurisdiction of the court without written consent of the court and BAIL BONDS, Inc., or its Agent.
    (b) If Defendant shall move from one address to another without notifying BAIL BONDS, Inc., or its Agent in writing prior to said move.
    (c) If Defendant shall commit any act which shall constitute reasonable evidence of Defendant's intention to cause a forfeiture of said bond.
    (d) If Defendant is arrested and incarcerated for any offense other than a minor traffic violation.
    (e) If Defendant shall make any material false statement in the application.

ALL INFORMATION BELOW MUST BE COMPLETED IN FULL, OR DELAY WILL OCCUR
(PLEASE PRINT)

NAME OF DEFENDANT _____ PHONE _____
FIRST _____ MIDDLE _____ LAST

NICKNAME OR ALIAS _____ RACE _____

RESIDENCE ADDRESS _____ CITY _____ ZIP _____ HOW LONG _____

PREVIOUS ADDRESS _____ CITY _____ ZIP _____ HOW LONG _____

OCCUPATION _____ EMPLOYED BY _____ HOW LONG _____

EMPLOYER'S ADDRESS _____ PHONE _____

PREVIOUS EMPLOYMENT _____ HOW LONG _____

DATE OF BIRTH _____ HEIGHT _____ WEIGHT _____ COLOR OF EYES _____ COLOR OF HAIR _____

IDENTIFICATION MARKS OR TATTOOS _____ SOCIAL SECURITY NO. _____

SPOUSE'S NAME _____ DATE OF BIRTH _____

EMPLOYED BY _____ ADDRESS _____ PHONE _____

CHILDREN'S NAMES	AGE	SCHOOL OR HOME ADDRESS

PERSONAL REFERENCES	WORK OR HOME ADDRESS	PHONE
1		
2		
3		

RELATIVES	STREET ADDRESS CITY AND STATE	PHONE
FATHER		
MOTHER		
BROTHER		
BROTHER		
SISTER		
SISTER		
FATHER-IN-LAW		
MOTHER-IN-LAW		
BROTHER-IN-LAW		
COUSIN		

PLEASE CONTINUE ON NEXT PAGE

DEFENDANT QUESTIONNAIRE (CONTINUED)

DEFENDANT'S ATTORNEY _____ ADDRESS _____ PHONE _____

INDEMNITOR'S NAME _____ INDEMNITOR'S RELATIONSHIP TO APPLICANT _____

INDEMNITOR'S ADDRESS _____ PHONE _____

INDEMNITOR'S EMPLOYER _____ ADDRESS _____ PHONE _____

DEFENDANT ARRESTED BEFORE _____ CONVICTED _____ OFFENSE _____ ON PAROLE ____ ON PROBATION ____

AUTOMOBILE — MAKE _____ MODEL _____ YEAR _____ COLOR _____ LICENSE NO. _____ STATE _____

WHEN AND WHERE DID YOU BUY CAR? _____ AMOUNT OWING _____ TO WHOM _____

DRIVER'S LICENSE NO. _____ STATE _____ DRAFT BOARD LOCATION _____

MILITARY SERVICE _____ WHAT BRANCH _____ HONORABLY DISCHARGED _____ WHEN _____

ARE YOU UNDER ANY BAIL BOND NOW _____ AGENT OR SURETY _____

REMARKS: _____
_____
_____

The Defendant hereby warrant(s) that the foregoing declarations made and answers given are the truth without reservation and are made for the purpose of inducing the Surety to become or to procure suretyship on the bond or undertaking applied for herein, with the intent and purpose that they be fully relied on.

In addition, the Defendant hereby authorizes and directs his relatives, employers, bankers, the Federal Social Security Administration, the Internal Revenue, the state Department of Disability Insurance, the United States Armed Forces, the State Division of Motor Vehicles, all Municipal, County, State and Federal Law Enforcement Agencies and any other persons or organizations having information concerning the Defendant's whereabouts to give such information to   BAIL BONDS, Inc.   and its assigns and/or duly authorized representatives. The Defendant understands that any information obtained will be used for the purpose of securing his or her appearance and/or apprehension for Court appearance, and for the purpose of securing reimbursement for any expenses incurred as a result of Defendant's non-appearance. The Defendant hereby waives his or her rights with respect to the Privacy Act and authorizes the use of copies of this document by Amwest Surety Insurance Company and its assigns and/or duly authorized representatives.

Signed, sealed and delivered this _____ day of _____ , 20 _____

DEFENDANT
SIGN HERE X _____   (SEAL)

                 SIGNATURE OF DEFENDANT

_____

                 MAILING ADDRESS

AGENT
WITNESS HERE _____

                 SIGNATURE OF AGENT

POWER OF ATTORNEY
Know All Men by These Presents

THAT I, _____

and by these presents do make, constitute and appoint _____

my true and lawful attorney for me and in my name, place and stead to act for me in the _____ Court of

_____ County, in connection with the charge of _____
now pending against me in said County; and to enter such a plea as he may feel is proper in connection with the said charge, giving and granting unto my said attorney full power and authority to do and perform all and every act and thing whatsoever requisite and necessary to be done in and about the premises as fully, to all intents and purposes, as I might or could do if personally present, with full power of substitution and revocation, hereby ratifying and confirming all that my said attorney or his substitute shall lawfully do or cause to be done by virtue hereof.

IN WITNESS WHEREOF, I have hereunto set my hand and seal this _____ day of _____ , 20 _____

STATE OF _____   X _____ (SEAL)
                                           (Signature of defendant)
COUNTY OF _____

On this _____ day of _____ , 20 _____ before me personally appeared _____

_____ to me known to be the person_____ described in and who

executed the foregoing instrument and _____ thereupon acknowledged to me that _____ executed the same.

_____
                 Notary Public

My Commission Expires _____

BAIL BONDS, Inc.

DEFENDANT _____

AGENT _____

POWER NO. _____

CAUSE NO. _____

EXECUTION DATE _____

FINANCIAL STATEMENT AND INDEMNITY AGREEMENT

NAME OF INDEMNITOR _____ FIRST ___ MIDDLE ___ LAST ___ PHONE _____ DATE OF BIRTH _____

RESIDENCE ADDRESS _____ CITY _____ ZIP _____

EMPLOYED BY _____ SOCIAL SECURITY NO. _____

EMPLOYER'S ADDRESS _____ PHONE _____

SPOUSE'S NAME _____ DATE OF BIRTH _____

EMPLOYED BY _____ ADDRESS _____ PHONE _____

PARENTS _____ ADDRESS _____

PERSONAL REFERENCES	WORK OR HOME ADDRESS	PHONE
1.		
2.		
3.		

	ASSETS	AMOUNT		LIABILITIES	AMOUNT
CASH	PRINCIPAL BANK—ADDRESS		NOTES PAYABLE TO BANKS	PRINCIPAL BANK — ADDRESS	
	Other Banks			Other	
STOCKS AND BONDS	Listed		OTHER NOTES AND ACCOUNTS PAYABLE	Real Estate Loans	
	Unlisted			Sales Contracts & Sec. Agreements	
				Loans on Life Insurance Policies	
REAL ESTATE	Improved				
	Unimproved		TAXES PAYABLE	Current Year's Income Taxes Unpaid	
	Trust Deeds and Mortgages			Prior Years' Income Taxes Unpaid	
				Real Estate Taxes Unpaid	
LIFE INSURANCE	Cash Surrender Value				
				Unpaid Interest	
ACCOUNTS AND NOTES RECEIVABLE	Relatives and Friends			Others	
	Collectible		OTHER LIABILITIES		
	Doubtful				
OTHER PERSONAL PROPERTY	Automobile			TOTAL LIABILITIES	
	Other			NET WORTH	
	TOTAL			TOTAL	

The maker of the above statement hereby authorizes the Surety to confirm the bank balances claimed and all other items comprising said statement.

Are you guarantor upon any other bonds? _____ Endorser upon any note or other obligation? _____ Are there any judgements against you? _____

Explain "yes" answers _____

_____

_____

YOU ARE ASSUMING SPECIFIC OBLIGATIONS — READ CAREFULLY?

WHEREAS, _____ BONDS, Inc., (hereinafter called the SURETY), at the request of or on behalf of the undersigned, has or is about to become on and appearance bond for _____

_____ Defendant

in the sum of _____ Dollars ($ _____) by its certain bond or undertaking, a copy of which is attached hereto and made a part hereof.

NOW THEREFORE, in consideration of the premises and the sum of one dollar in hand paid, receipt whereof be each of us is hereby acknowledged, the undersigned jointly and severally do hereby undertake, agree and bind themselves their legal representatives, successors and assigns, as follows on reverse side hereof:

1. That the undersigned will have the aforesaid _____ forthcoming before the above court named in said bond, attached hereto, at the time therein fixed and from day to day and term thereafter, as may be ordered by the said court.

2. That the undersigned will at all times indemnify and save the said SURETY harmless from and against every and all claims, demands, liabilities, costs, charges, counsel fees, expense, suits, orders, judgements, or adjudications whatsoever which the said SURETY shall or may for any cause at any time sustain or incur, by reason or in consequence of the said SURETY having executed said bond or undertaking, will, upon demand, place the said SURETY in funds to meet all such claims, demands, liabilities, costs, charges, counsel fees, expenses, suits, order, judgements, or adjudications against it, by reason of such SURETY-ship, and before the said SURETY shall be required to pay the same.

3. That the agreement of indemnity contained in paragraph 2 above shall continue as long as the SURETY has any liability or has sustained any loss, upon the bond referred to herein, and the undersigned further agrees not to make any transfer, or any attempted transfer of any of the property, real or personal, in which the undersigned has as interest or in which the undersigned may subsequently acquire any interest, and its further agreed that the SURETY shall have a lien upon all property of the undersigned for any sums due it or for which it has become, or may become, liable by reason of its having executed the bond referred to herein. It is further agreed that the Indemnity Agreement contained in Paragraph 2 above and the provisions of this paragraph shall be binding upon and apply to any subsidiary, affiliate, parent or related enterprises created or acquired by the undersigned.

4. That the voucher or other evidence of any payment made by the said SURETY, by reason of such surety-ship, shall be conclusive evidence of such payment against the undersigned, the successors and assigns of the undersigned, as well as the estate of the undersigned, and those entitled the share in the estate of the undersigned as to both the property thereof and as to the extent of the liability thereunder of the said SURETY.

5. That the said SURETY may withdraw from its Surety-ship upon said bond or undertaking at any time it may see fit, as provided by law.

6. That the undersigned's liability hereunder shall apply not only to the bond referred to above, but shall apply to all other bonds or undertakings which may at any time be issued by the SURETY at the request of or on behalf of the undersigned.

7. That the agreement shall not be returned by the said SURETY at the time it shall be satisfied of the termination of its liability under said bond or obligation, but shall be retained as security for any liability that may at any time thereafter occur.

8. That the failure of any of the undersigned to comply with the provisions of this agreement of indemnity shall be binding upon the others.

9. If any provision or provisions of this instrument be void or unforceable under the laws of any place governing its construction or enforcement, this instrument shall not be void or vitiated thereby but shall be construed and enforced with the same effect as though such provision were omitted.

WITNESSES:

_____   X _____
                                                         SIGNATURE OF DEFENDANT

_____   X _____
                                                         SIGNATURE OF INDEMNITOR

_____   X _____
                                                         SIGNATURE OF CO-INDEMNITOR

STATE OF _____

COUNTY OF _____

On this _____ day of _____ 20 _____ before me personally appeared _____
_____ to me known to be the person _____ described in and who
executed the foregoing instrument and _____ thereupon acknowledged to me that _____ executed the same _____

_____
                                              Notary Public

My Commission Expires _____

PROMISSORY NOTE

$ _____ _____ _____ 20 _____
                                                     City and State

On demand after date, for value received _____ Promise to pay to the order of

BONDS, Inc. or its Agent
_____

_____ DOLLARS,

at _____ with interest

thereon at the rate of _____ per cent, per annum from Call Date until fully paid. Interest payable semi-annually. The maker and endorser of this note further agree to waive demand, notice of non-payment and protest; and in case suit shall be brought for the collection hereof, or the same has to be collected upon demand of an attorney, to pay reasonable attorney's fees

for making such collection. Deferred interest payments to bear interest from maturity at _____ per cent, per annum, payable semi-annually.

It is further agreed and specifically understood that this note shall become Null and Void in the event the said

defendant _____
shall appear in the proper court at the time or times so directed by the Judge or Judges of competent jurisdiction until the obligations under the appearance bond or bonds posted on behalf of the defendant have been fulfilled **and the Surety discharged of all liability thereunder,** otherwise to remain in full force and effect.

_____ (Seal)

Date _____ 20 _____   _____ (Seal)

ASSIGNMENT OF SAVINGS ACCOUNT/CERTIFICATE OF DEPOSIT

Know All Persons by These Presents: For value received, and as collateral security on a bond or bonds described as follows:

the undersigned hereby assigns, transfers and conveys unto

its _____ No. _____ in _____
Name of Depository

at _____
Address of Depository

to the extent of $ _____ of said account, and as further evidence thereof there is being delivere

contemporaneously herewith the original _____ of the undersigned in said Depository together with a d
executed withdrawal order for the said amount hereinbefore assigned. The Depository is hereby ordered to pay the entire proceeds of sa
account to _____ upon its demand, and the undersigned hereby waives any and all right of recou
against the Depository in connection with any such payment.

This Assignment is executed in duplicate and it shall remain in full force and effect until the said
_____ ully indemnified and reimbursed for all loss, cost and expense, and until all liability has
minated, upon the bond or bonds hereinbefore described. No change or termination of this agreement shall be valid unless consent
to in writing by

Dated _____

_____
Owner

State of _____)
County of _____) ss.

_____
Owner

On this _____ day of _____ , in the year 19 ____, before me, the undersigned

Notary Public in and for said County and State, personally appeared _____

_____ personally known to me (or proved to me on the basis of satisfact
evidence) to be the person(s) whose name(s) is subscribed to this instrument, and acknowledged that ____ he ____ executed it.

_____
Notary Public

ACCEPTANCE OF NOTICE BY DEPOSITORY

The undersigned Depository acknowledges receipt of the foregoing assignment, and agrees that its rights to any offset against this acco

are waived, and agrees to abide by its terms, this _____ day of _____

19 ____ at _____ o'clock, _____ M.

```
+--------------------------------+
|                                |
|     AFFIX DEPOSITORY STAMP     |
|                                |
|                                |
|                                |
|                                |
+--------------------------------+
```

_____
Name of Depository

By: _____

_____
Title of Officer

MORGAGE

At the request of _____ (the undersigned),
who reside(s) at _____
and upon the security hereof,   **BAIL BONDS, INC. (Surety)** with an address of
_____ has arranged, executed or continued an appearance bond, executed
on _____ (date), for _____ (Principal).

Said appearance bond was executed in the sum of $ _____ dollars and was posted in
a District/Superior Court in the State of Vermont/New Hampshire.

For ten dollars ($10.00) and other good and valuable consideration, the receipt and sufficiency of
which is hereby acknowledged, the undersigned (jointly and severally if more than one) absolutely and
unconditionally covenant, promise, undertake, agree and bind themselves, their representatives, successors,
heirs and assigns as follows:

1. The undersigned shall have the Principal forthcoming before the Court named in said bond, or in
    the event of a bindover, the Court to which bound, at the time therein fixed, or as provided by law,
    and from day to day and term to term thereafter as may be ordered by such Court.
2. The undersigned shall at all times indemnify and hold harmless the Surety from and against every
    loss, cost and expense which the Surety shall or may for any cause at any time directly or
    indirectly sustain or incur by reason or consequence of the execution or continuation of said bond
    and every bond executed in substitution for said bond, with or without the consent of the
    undersigned. This indemnity shall include (but not be limited to) bond estreatures and forfeitures,
    judgments, court costs, sheriff's fees, attorney's fees and appellate attorney fees, suits, orders and
    adjudications, recording and filing fees, reward offerings, investigative expenses reasonably
    incurred in the attempt to locate the Principal, and incidental expenses incurred in the Principal's
    apprehension and return to custody. The undersigned shall place the Surety in funds to meet every
    such loss, cost and expense before the Surety is required to pay the same.
3. The undersigned guarantee the payment of every premium on the bond(s) described above
    promptly without first requiring the Surety or Sureties to proceed against the Principal.
4. To secure the payment and performance of every obligation described herein, the undersigned
    hereby grant, convey and mortgage to the Surety, all of the following described property together
    with all appurtenances thereto:

5. The undersigned fully warrant fee simple title to said property, shall pay all obligations of every
    nature thereon promptly when due, and shall defend the same against the claims and demands of
    all persons. The undersigned shall insure said property in form and amount satisfactory to the
    Surety with a loss payable clause in favor of the Surety.
6. If any sum referred to herein remains unpaid for ten (10) days after the same becomes due, such
    payment shall be considered in default and bear interest at the highest rate allowed by law. The
    Surety or Sureties may then foreclose this agreement, notwithstanding any exemption that may be
    available by law, and shall be entitled to recover forthwith any deficiency which may occur.
7. The undersigned waive all notices and demands and shall pay all costs of collection incurred by
    the Surety in connection herewith, whether suit be brought or not, including attorney fees,
    appellate attorney fees and collection agency fees. The Surety may discuss any default with the
    present or future employers of the undersigned.
8. The term "Surety" shall include the Surety above named and every Surety Company on the
    bond(s) referred to herein and their agents, co-sureties, re-insurers, successors and assigns. The

rights given to the Surety herein shall be in addition to any rights that the Surety may have under separate agreements or applicable law.

9. The acquiescence of the Surety in any default by the undersigned shall not constitute a waiver of such default. If any provision of this agreement is void or unenforceable under law, this agreement shall not be void but shall be construed and enforced as though such provision was omitted. The singular form used herein shall include the plural form, where applicable, and vice versa.

10. The Surety is authorized to secure an investigative consumer report and information from any credit reporting agency or other source pertaining to the undersigned's character and/or financial condition whether the undersigned is in default or not. Every person, firm and corporation furnishing the Surety with information in good faith is hereby released from all damages and liability.

11. Any default of any mortgage on any property pledged as collateral on this bond(s) shall permit the Surety to surrender the Principal without return of premium.

12. *This instrument depends upon the happening of a contingency before an obligation to pay is created. Payment shall become due upon demand in the event of a forfeiture of the above referenced bond(s).*

13. For property located in the State of Vermont, a Power of Sale to foreclose this mortgage pursuant to the provisions of Vermont Statutes Annotated Title 12 Sections 4531 through 4533, is hereby granted.

14. This mortgage is upon the statutory conditions, for any breach of which the Surety shall have the statutory power of sale. All Homestead Rights are waived.

SIGNED, SEALED and DELIVERED at _____ , State of _____ , this _____ day of _____ , 20_____ .

Witness: _____   X _____ (L.S.)
Print: _____   Print Name: _____

Witness: _____   X _____ (L.S.)
Print: _____   Print Name: _____

STATE OF _____
COUNTY OF _____ AT _____

     I hereby certify that on this day, before me, an officer duly authorized to administer oaths and take acknowledgements, personally appeared _____
_____ known to me to be the person(s) described herein and who executed the foregoing instrument, who acknowledged before me that they executed the same, and that an oath was taken.

WITNESS MY HAND and official seal this _____ day of _____ , 20___ .

                    Before Me _____
                             Notary Public/Justice of the Peace

Bail Bonds, Inc.
Bail Bonds

Receipt for Collateral Deposited

Received From (Depositor) _____ Date _____

Address _____

As collateral for the appearance of (Defendant) _____

The following described property is collateral for a bail bond in the amount of $ _____

_____

I acknowledge that this collateral could be forfeited in the event of the non-appearance (failure to appear in court) of the defendant named above. In addition, I acknowledge that I may be liable for cost beyond the amount of the collateral for the apprehension of the defendant or for the payment of forfeited bail by 3ail Bonds, Inc.

IMPORTANT NOTES: (1) Collateral will only be returned when the criminal case is completed and a discharge has been received from the court by   Bail Bonds, Inc.   Bail Bonds. (2) Collateral will only be returned to the depositor named above. (3) Since collateral is returned by mail, you must inform   Bail Bonds, Inc.'   Bail Bonds by mail of any change of address. (4) Collateral paid by credit card will only be returned by a credit to your credit card. If you cancel your credit card, inform   3ail Bonds, Inc.   Bail Bonds by mail immediately.

Bail Agent X _____ Depositor X _____

Receipt for Non-Refundable Payment of Fees and Expenses

Received from _____ Date _____

Address _____

The following are *Non-Refundable* Fees and Expenses for a bail bond of $ _____

Bail Bond Fee: $_____ Expenses: $_____ Total: $_____ . Bond #_____

Defendant's Name _____

The defendant's next court appearance is _____ at _____ AM/PM in the following court:

_____ to answer to the charge of _____.

Bail Agent X _____ Received by X _____

State of New Hampshire

_____ County   _____ Court

                                                          _____ Tel. #

State v. [   ]   D.O.B. _____   _____ No.

Offense(s) Charged: _____

_____   Police Dept. _____

_____   Date of Offense: _____

BOND IN CRIMINAL CASE

Received of _____   Amount $ [   ]

☐ **CASH BAIL / CORPORATE SURETY BAIL BOND** to secure defendant's compliance with the Conditions of Bail written below.

*   *   *

☐ **PERSONAL RECOGNIZANCE** The defendant agrees s/he is indebted to the State of New Hampshire in the amount of $ _____ Personal Recognizance Bail to secure defendant's compliance with the Conditions of Bail written below.

CONDITIONS OF BAIL

1. The defendant shall appear in this court to answer this charge at _____ M. _____
   on [   ]

2. The defendant shall appear in any New Hampshire Court to answer this charge when notified to report to the court.
3. The defendant immediately shall notify any New Hampshire Court in which this case is pending of any change of address.
4. The defendant shall keep the peace and be of good behavior.
5. Other:

    If the defendant complies with the Conditions of Bail, this obligation shall be null and void on final disposition of this charge.
    If the defendant does not comply with any condition(s) Cash Bail shall be forfeited to the State surety or surety and execution may issue against the defendant for Personal Recognizance and against the Corporate surety or surety. In addition, the court may order the arrest of the defendant.

Date: _____   _____
                                          DEFENDANT

Time: _____   Address _____

_____   _____
BAIL COMMISSIONER/CLERK OF COURT

                                          _____
                                          CORPORATE SURETY or SURETY

Bail Commissioner's fee $ _____   Address _____

                                          _____

AOC-110-245-2/86   **BAIL BOND**

STATE OF VERMONT

District Court of Vermont

APPEARANCE BOND

State
v.

Bail Bond Power Number: _____

Defendant	Unit No.	County/Circuit	Docket No.

Address	Offense

I am the defendant in this case, and I reside at the address filled in above. By my signature, I agree to appear at all court proceedings scheduled in this case for which I or my attorney received notice. I understand that if I fail to appear or violate any other conditions of my release the court may issue a warrant for my arrest. I also understand that failure to appear at a scheduled court proceeding or as otherwise required by the conditions of my release can result in imprisonment of not more than two years and a fine of not more than $5,000 under 13 V.S.A. 7559 (d).

In addition, I agree to the following order to secure my release pending trial in this case:

☐ 1. I have been given a copy of the conditions of my release and agree to obey all the conditions listed. I understand that an alleged violation may cause the court to issue an immediate summons for a violation hearing.

☐ 2. I understand and agree that if I do not appear at a scheduled court proceeding for which I or my attorney have received notice, I must pay the State of Vermont the sum of $ _____, which is the amount of the bond.

☐ 3. I have deposited $ _____ with the Clerk of the Vermont District Court.

I understand that if I obey all the conditions of my release and appear before this Court when I am ordered to do so, then this appearance bond will be void and any deposit will be returned to me. I also understand that any deposit will not be returned until this case is closed and I surrender myself to serve any sentence I may receive, or until further order of the court.

Witness	Date

Witness	Defendant's Signature

I/we the undersigned do hereby voluntarily agree to act as surety for the above named defendant, in order to secure his/her release pending trial. I/we understand that the purpose of this appearance bond is to insure the attendance of the defendant at all court ordered proceedings, and that as surety it is my/our responsibility to know when and where the defendant is to appear.

In addition, I/we agree to the following:

☐ 1. If the defendant fails to appear at a scheduled court proceeding I/we will be liable to the State of Vermont for $ _____, which is the amount of the bond.

☐ 2. I have deposited $ _____ with the Clerk of the Vermont District Court.

I/we understand that if the defendant obeys all the conditions of his/her release and appears before the Court when ordered to do so then this appearance bond will be void and any deposit returned. I also understand that any deposit will not be returned until this case is closed and the defendant surrenders him/herself to serve any sentence that may be imposed, or until further order of the Court.

I/we further understand that if I/we should ever become concerned about the above responsibilities, the defendant may be surrendered to the Court and bail returned according to Title 13 V.S.A. section 7562.

Date	Signature/Surety	

Date	Signature/Surety	
	Agent, Attorney-In-Fact	

Witness	Witness

Form No. 344

STATE OF VERMONT
CONDITIONS OF RELEASE ORDER

Docket Number

Defendant	D.O.B.	Unit	Circuit	Offense

The Court has determined that future appearance(s) of the defendant will not be reasonably assured by his/her release on personal recognizance or execution of an unsecured appearance bond alone; and that the release of the defendant will constitute a danger to the public. It is therefore ordered that the defendant be released upon the following marked conditions:

1. ☐ THE DEFENDANT SHALL PERSONALLY APPEAR IN COURT AS REQUIRED BY NOTICE TO THE DEFENDANT OR DEFENDANT'S ATTORNEY, OR BE IN VIOLATION OF THIS ORDER.

2. ☐ Defendant shall let his/her attorney or the court clerk know where s/he is at all times, and a telephone number and address where s/he may be reached.

3. ☐ Defendant shall not be charged with, and have probable cause found for, a felony, a crime against a person, or an offense like the offense s/he is now charged with.

4. ☐ Defendant is released into the custody of

5. ☐ Defendant shall report to

6. ☐ Defendant shall reside in _____ County and shall not travel outside of that County without written permission from this Court.

7. ☐ Defendant shall not operate a motor vehicle.

8. ☐ Defendant shall not operate a motor vehicle unless legally authorized to do so, and in possession of a valid motor vehicle operator's license.

9. ☐ Defendant shall execute an appearance bond in the amount of $ _____ , and deposit 10% of this amount in cash.

10. ☐ Defendant shall execute a bail bond with sufficient sureties, or deposit cash in the amount of $ _____ .

11. ☐ Defendant shall observe the following curfew conditions:

12. ☐ Defendant shall not purchase, possess, or consume any alcoholic beverages.

13. ☐ Defendant shall not purchase, possess, or use any firearms.

14. ☐ Defendant shall not associate with _____ nor personally contact, harass, or cause to be harassed _____

15. ☐ Defendant shall appear in the District Court named above on _____ at _____ .

16. ☐ Defendant shall be subject to arrest without warrant pursuant to V.R.Cr.P.3(a)(b) if s/he does not appear as directed in Condition(s) No. _____ without just cause.

17. ☐ The following additional conditions are imposed on the defendant:

By Order of the Court: (Please see additional information on the back)

Presiding Judge/Clerk	Date

I have received a copy of this order. I have read it. I understand it.

Defendant	Date

R 5M 3/89 Quad Set 25 per pad V.C.1.

| 1st Copy - Court | 2nd Copy - Defendant | 3rd Copy - State's Atty. | 4th Copy - Arresting Dept |

Appendix

1. <u>Limited Power Of Attorney</u> – When a surety insurance company appoints you as their representative, they will provide you with this Limited Power of Attorney, which you give to the regulating authority in your state. This POA is official notification that you represent the company, and shows the maximum amount that you can bind the company on any one bail bond.

2. <u>Court Bond</u> – This bond is an example of related business that you can develop from your bail bond business. American Contractors Indemnity Corporation, a division of HCC Surety Group www.hccsurety.com, posted this bond. A very active player in the bail business, HCC has urged its agents to explore the court bond business. In this situation, a bond was written for $30 million, with a premium of $938,000, of which about 20% was paid to the agent.

3. <u>IRS Form 8300</u> – The Internal Revenue Service requires this two-page form whenever you receive more than $10,000 in cash (which will happen more often than you think!). To avoid nasty investigations, be sure to use this form regularly.

B 14427

No Power of Attorney on this form shall be valid as to bonds, undertakings, recognizances or other written obligations in the nature thereof executed on or after said expiration date.

Amwest
Amwest Surety Insurance Company
P.O. Box 4500, Woodland Hills, CA 91365-4500

Tel: (818) 704-044

NAME OF PRINCIPAL: **RICHARD VERROCHI**

NAME OF OBLIGEE: **HILLSBORO COUNTY**

This Power of Attorney may not be used in conjunction with any other power of attorney. This Power of Attorney is void if altered or erased. This document is printed on white paper with black and red ink. This Power of Attorney bears a facsimile seal of **AMWEST SURETY INSURANCE COMPANY**. Only originals of this Power of Attorney are valid. No representations or warranties regarding this Power of Attorney may be made by any person other than an authorized officer of **AMWEST SURETY INSURANCE COMPANY**, and must be in writing. Questions or inquiries regarding this Power of Attorney must be addressed to **AMWEST SURETY INSURANCE COMPANY** at the address and telephone number set forth at the top of this Power of Attorney, attention: Court Division. This Power of Attorney shall be governed by the laws of the State of California. Any power of attorney used in connection with any bail bond issued by **AMWEST SURETY INSURANCE COMPANY** on or after March 1, 1992 must be on Amwest forms BB-A1011 (3/92) or BB-A1012 (3/92). All other previous power of attorney forms issued by **AMWEST SURETY INSURANCE COMPANY** have been revoked and have no further force or effect.

KNOW ALL MEN BY THESE PRESENTS that **AMWEST SURETY INSURANCE COMPANY**, A CALIFORNIA CORPORATION, (the Company), does hereby make, constitute and appoint

RICHARD VERROCHI

its true and lawful Attorney(s) In Fact, with limited power and authority for and on behalf of the Company as Surety to execute and deliver and affix the seal of the Company thereto if a seal is required on bonds, undertakings, recognizances or other written obligations in the nature thereof, as follows:

ALL BAIL BONDS UP TO AND INCLUDING
FIFTY-THOUSAND DOLLARS ($50,000.00)

and to bind **AMWEST SURETY INSURANCE COMPANY** thereby. This appointment is made under and by authority of the following provisions of the By-Laws of the Company, which are now in full force and effect:

Article III, Section 7 of the By-Law of **AMWEST SURETY INSURANCE COMPANY**

This Power of Attorney is signed and sealed by facsimile under and by the authority of the following resolutions adopted by the Board of Directors of **AMWEST SURETY INSURANCE COMPANY** at a meeting duly held on December 15, 1975.

RESOLVED that the president or any officer, in conjunction with the secretary or any assistant secretary, may appoint an attorney-in-fact or agents with authority as defined or limited in the instrument evidencing the appointment in each case, for and on behalf of the Company to execute and deliver and affix the seal of the Company to bonds, undertakings, recognizances, and suretyship obligations of all kinds; and said officers may remove any such attorney-in-fact or agent and revoke any power of attorney previously granted to such person.

RESOLVED FURTHER that any bond, undertaking, recognizance, or suretyship obligation shall be valid and binding upon the Company

(i) when signed by the president or any officer and attested and sealed (if a seal be required) by any secretary or assistant secretary; or

(ii) when signed by the president or any officer or secretary or assistant secretary, and countersigned and sealed (if a seal be required) by a duly authorized attorney-in-fact or agent; or

(iii) when duly executed and sealed (if a seal be required) by one or more attorneys-in-fact or agents pursuant to and within the limits of the authority evidenced by the power of attorney issued by the Company to such person or persons.

RESOLVED FURTHER that the signature of any authorized officer and the seal of the Company may be affixed by facsimile to any power of attorney or certification thereof authorizing the execution and delivery of any bond, undertaking, recognizance, or other suretyship obligations of the Company; and such signature and seal when so used shall have the same force and effect as though manually affixed.

IN WITNESS WHEREOF, **AMWEST SURETY INSURANCE COMPANY** has caused these presents to be signed by its proper officers, and its corporate seal to be hereunto affixed this _____**27th**_____ day of _____**March**_____ 19 **92**

Arthur F. Melton - Senior Vice President

Andrea I. Shapiro - Assistant Secretary

State of California

County of **Los Angeles**

On **March 27, 1992** before me, _____ **Tammy L. Zeigler** _____ (here insert name) Notary

Public, personally appeared _____ **Arthur F. Melton and Andrea I. Shapiro** _____, personally known to me (or proved to me on the basis of satisfactory evidence) to be the person(s) whose name(s) is/are subscribed to the within instrument and acknowledged to me all that he/she/they executed the same in his/her/their authorized capacity(ies), and that by his/her/their signature(s) on the instrument the person(s), or the entity upon behalf of which the person(s) acted, executed the instrument.

WITNESS my hand and official seal.

Signature _____

(Seal)

OFFICIAL SEAL
TAMMY L. ZEIGLER
NOTARY PUBLIC - CALIFORNIA
LOS ANGELES COUNTY
My Comm. Expires July 21, 1995

CERTIFICATE

I, the undersigned, assistant secretary of the **AMWEST SURETY INSURANCE COMPANY**, a California corporation, DO HEREBY CERTIFY that the foregoing and attached Power of Attorney remains in full force and has not been revoked, and furthermore, that the provisions of the By-Laws of the Company and the Resolutions of the Board of Directors set forth in the Power of Attorney, are now in force.

Signed and sealed at **Woodland Hills, CA** this **6th** day of **January** 19 **94**

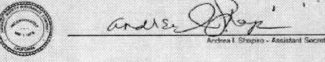

Andrea I. Shapiro - Assistant Secretary

A BB-A1011 (5/92) Ω

American Contractors Indemnity Company

In the ___Superior___ Court
County of ___Los Angeles___ State of California

ROMOLA ROBINS, individually and as trustee of the ROBINS FAMILY TRUST, et al.)	
)	
Plaintiff)	
)	
vs.)	
)	Case No. ___LC 068574___
ANTON ROLAND, as an individual, a) s trustee of the ROLAND FAMILY TRUST, et al)	
)	UNDERTAKING UNDER
Defendants)	SECTION ___917.1___ C.C.P.
)	American Contractors Indemnity Company
AND RELATED CROSS ACTION.)	9841 Airport Blvd., 9th Floor
)	Los Angeles, CA 90045
)	
)	

WHEREAS, the above named Anton Roland, Roland Land Company, Roland Enterprises, Roland Land Investment Co., Inc., Roland Land Investment & Development, California Resources Enterprises, Inc., Consolidated Land Associates, Roland Heights Development, Inc., Roland Universal Land Co. Inc., C.G.M.V, Inc., George Roland and Cathy Roland Thompson ___ desires to

give an undertaking for ___Appeal___ as provided in
Section ___917.1___ C.C.P.

NOW THEREFORE, the undersigned Surety, does hereby obligate itself, jointly and severally, to ___Romola Robins and___
___Philip Vardi___ under said
statutory obligations in the sum of ___****************************Thirty Million Dollars****************************___
___ Dollars ($___30,000,000.00___).

Leon B. Back, Jr.
IN WITNESS WHEREOF, The corporate seal and name of the said Surety Company is hereto affixed and attested by
___ who declares under penalty of perjury that he is its duly authorized Attorney-in-Fact acting under an
unrevoked power of attorney on file with the Clerk of the County in which above entitled Court is located.

Executed at ___Los Angeles___, California on ___June 9, 2006___

Bond No. ___294579___ AMERICAN CONTRACTORS INDEMNITY COMPANY

The premium charge for this bond is
$ ___938,000.00___ per annum. Attorney-in-Fact ___Leon B. Back, Jr.___

IRS Form **8300**
(Rev. December 2004)
OMB No. 1545-0892
Department of the Treasury
Internal Revenue Service

Report of Cash Payments Over $10,000
Received in a Trade or Business
▶ See instructions for definition of cash.

▶ Use this form for transactions occurring after December 31, 2004. Do not use prior versions after this date.

For Privacy Act and Paperwork Reduction Act Notice, see page 5.

FinCEN Form **8300**
(Rev. December 2004)
OMB No. 1506-0018
Department of the Treasury
Financial Crimes
Enforcement Network

1 Check appropriate box(es) if: **a** ☐ Amends prior report; **b** ☐ Suspicious transaction.

Part I   Identity of Individual From Whom the Cash Was Received

2 If more than one individual is involved, check here and see instructions . . . . ▶ ☐

3 Last name	**4** First name	**5** M.I.	**6** Taxpayer identification number

7 Address (number, street, and apt. or suite no.)	**8** Date of birth ▶ (see instructions) M M D D Y Y Y Y

9 City	**10** State	**11** ZIP code	**12** Country (if not U.S.)	**13** Occupation, profession, or business

14 Identifying document (ID)	**a Describe ID** ▶ .... **c Number** ▶	**b Issued by** ▶ ....

Part II   Person on Whose Behalf This Transaction Was Conducted

15 If this transaction was conducted on behalf of more than one person, check here and see instructions . . . . ▶ ☐

16 Individual's last name or Organization's name	**17** First name	**18** M.I.	**19** Taxpayer identification number

20 Doing business as (DBA) name (see instructions)	Employer identification number

21 Address (number, street, and apt. or suite no.)	**22** Occupation, profession, or business

23 City	**24** State	**25** ZIP code	**26** Country (if not U.S.)

27 Alien identification (ID)	**a Describe ID** ▶ .... **c Number** ▶	**b Issued by** ▶ ....

Part III   Description of Transaction and Method of Payment

28 Date cash received M M D D Y Y Y Y	**29** Total cash received $ .00	**30** If cash was received in more than one payment, check here . . . ▶ ☐	**31** Total price if different from item 29 $ .00

32 Amount of cash received (in U.S. dollar equivalent) (must equal item 29) (see instructions):

- **a** U.S. currency $ _____ .00 (Amount in $100 bills or higher $ _____ .00)
- **b** Foreign currency $ _____ .00 (Country ▶ _____)
- **c** Cashier's check(s) $ _____ .00   Issuer's name(s) and serial number(s) of the monetary instrument(s) ▶
- **d** Money order(s) $ _____ .00   ....
- **e** Bank draft(s) $ _____ .00   ....
- **f** Traveler's check(s) $ _____ .00

33 Type of transaction

- **a** ☐ Personal property purchased
- **b** ☐ Real property purchased
- **c** ☐ Personal services provided
- **d** ☐ Business services provided
- **e** ☐ Intangible property purchased
- **f** ☐ Debt obligations paid
- **g** ☐ Exchange of cash
- **h** ☐ Escrow or trust funds
- **i** ☐ Bail received by court clerks
- **j** ☐ Other (specify in item 34) ▶

34 Specific description of property or service shown in 33. Give serial or registration number, address, docket number, etc. ▶ ....

Part IV   Business That Received Cash

35 Name of business that received cash	**36** Employer identification number

37 Address (number, street, and apt. or suite no.)	Social security number

38 City	**39** State	**40** ZIP code	**41** Nature of your business

42 Under penalties of perjury, I declare that to the best of my knowledge the information I have furnished above is true, correct, and complete.

Signature ▶ _____ Authorized official   Title ▶ _____

43 Date of signature M M D D Y Y Y Y	**44** Type or print name of contact person	**45** Contact telephone number ( )

IRS Form **8300** (Rev. 12-2004)   Cat. No. 62133S   FinCEN Form **8300** (Rev. 12-2004)

Multiple Parties
(Complete applicable parts below if box 2 or 15 on page 1 is checked)

Part I   Continued—Complete if box 2 on page 1 is checked

3 Last name	4 First name	5 M.I.	6 Taxpayer identification number
7 Address (number, street, and apt. or suite no.)	8 Date of birth (see instructions) ▶		M M D D Y Y Y Y
9 City	10 State	11 ZIP code	12 Country (if not U.S.)	13 Occupation, profession, or business
14 Identifying document (ID)	a Describe ID ▶ .... c Number ▶		b Issued by ▶ ....

3 Last name	4 First name	5 M.I.	6 Taxpayer identification number
7 Address (number, street, and apt. or suite no.)	8 Date of birth (see instructions) ▶		M M D D Y Y Y Y
9 City	10 State	11 ZIP code	12 Country (if not U.S.)	13 Occupation, profession, or business
14 Identifying document (ID)	a Describe ID ▶ .... c Number ▶		b Issued by ▶ ....

Part II   Continued—Complete if box 15 on page 1 is checked

16 Individual's last name or Organization's name	17 First name	18 M.I.	19 Taxpayer identification number
20 Doing business as (DBA) name (see instructions)			Employer identification number
21 Address (number, street, and apt. or suite no.)		22 Occupation, profession, or business	
23 City	24 State	25 ZIP code	26 Country (if not U.S.)
27 Alien identification (ID)	a Describe ID ▶ .... c Number ▶		b Issued by ▶ ....

16 Individual's last name or Organization's name	17 First name	18 M.I.	19 Taxpayer identification number
20 Doing business as (DBA) name (see instructions)			Employer identification number
21 Address (number, street, and apt. or suite no.)		22 Occupation, profession, or business	
23 City	24 State	25 ZIP code	26 Country (if not U.S.)
27 Alien identification (ID)	a Describe ID ▶ .... c Number ▶		b Issued by ▶ ....

Comments – Please use the lines provided below to comment on or clarify any information you entered on any line in Parts I, II, III, and IV

_____

_____

_____

_____

Printed in the United States
86286LV00006B/54/A

9 780978 956912